AF293127

Marx Hardy Machiavelli Chesterton Cooper Emerson Joyce Austen
Defoe Abbott Melville Montaigne Haggard Hugo Eliot Grimm
Stoker Carroll Christie Maupassant Byron Molière Schiller
Wilde Garnett Fitzgerald Engels Smith Kafka
Goethe Einstein Hawthorne Hall
Cotton Dostoyevsky Willis
Baum Henry Kipling Doyle
Leslie Dumas Flaubert Nietzsche Balzac
Stockton Turgenev
Burroughs Vatsyayana Crane
Curtis Tocqueville Verne
Homer Widger Tolstoy Whitman Gogol Vinci
Darwin Thoreau Busch
Potter Freud Zola Twain Scott Plato Harte
Kant Jowett Stevenson Lawrence Dickens Burton Hesse
Andersen Cervantes
London Descartes Voltaire
Poe Aristotle Wells Cooke
Hale James Hastings
Bunner Shakespeare Irving
Richter Chekhov Chambers
Doré da Shaw Benedict Alcott
Dante Pushkin
Swift Wodehouse Newton

tredition

tredition was established in 2006 by Sandra Latusseck and Soenke Schulz. Based in Hamburg, Germany, tredition offers publishing solutions to authors and publishing houses, combined with worldwide distribution of printed and digital book content. tredition is uniquely positioned to enable authors and publishing houses to create books on their own terms and without conventional manufacturing risks.

For more information please visit: www.tredition.com

TREDITION CLASSICS

This book is part of the TREDITION CLASSICS series. The creators of this series are united by passion for literature and driven by the intention of making all public domain books available in printed format again - worldwide. Most TREDITION CLASSICS titles have been out of print and off the bookstore shelves for decades. At tredition we believe that a great book never goes out of style and that its value is eternal. Several mostly non-profit literature projects provide content to tredition. To support their good work, tredition donates a portion of the proceeds from each sold copy. As a reader of a TREDITION CLASSICS book, you support our mission to save many of the amazing works of world literature from oblivion. See all available books at www.tredition.com.

 Project Gutenberg

The content for this book has been graciously provided by Project Gutenberg. Project Gutenberg is a non-profit organization founded by Michael Hart in 1971 at the University of Illinois. The mission of Project Gutenberg is simple: To encourage the creation and distribution of eBooks. Project Gutenberg is the first and largest collection of public domain eBooks.

Stephen Arnold Douglas

William Garrott Brown

Imprint

This book is part of TREDITION CLASSICS

Author: William Garrott Brown
Cover design: Buchgut, Berlin – Germany

Publisher: tredition GmbH, Hamburg - Germany
ISBN: 978-3-8472-1396-3

www.tredition.com
www.tredition.de

The Riverside Biographical Series

–––––

1. ANDREW JACKSON, by W.G. Brown.

2. JAMES B. EADS, by Louis How.

3. BENJAMIN FRANKLIN, by Paul E. More.

4. PETER COOPER, by R.W. Raymond.

5. THOMAS JEFFERSON, by H.C. Merwin.

6. WILLIAM PENN, by George Hodges.

7. GENERAL GRANT, by Walter Allen.

8. LEWIS AND CLARK, by William R. Lighton.

9. JOHN MARSHALL, by James B. Thayer.

10. ALEXANDER HAMILTON, by Chas. A. Conant.

11. WASHINGTON IRVING, by H.W. Boynton.

12. PAUL JONES, by Hutchins Hapgood.

13. STEPHEN A. DOUGLAS, by W.G. Brown.

14. SAMUEL DE CHAMPLAIN, by H.D. Sedgwick, Jr.

Each about 140 pages, 16mo, with photogravure
portrait, 65 cents, *net*; *School Edition*, each,
50 cents, *net*.

HOUGHTON, MIFFLIN & CO.
Boston and New York

The Riverside Biographical Series

NUMBER 13

STEPHEN ARNOLD DOUGLAS

BY

WILLIAM GARROTT BROWN

STEPHEN ARNOLD DOUGLAS

BY

WILLIAM GARROTT BROWN

BOSTON AND NEW YORK
HOUGHTON, MIFFLIN AND COMPANY
The Riverside Press, Cambridge
1902

Published March, 1902

To J.S. Jr.

CHAPTER I

YOUTH AND THE WEST

The ten years of American history from 1850 to 1860 have a fascination second only to that of the four years which followed. Indeed, unless one has a taste for military science, it is a question whether the great war itself is more absorbing than the great debate that led up to it; whether even Gettysburg and Chickamauga, the March to the Sea, the Wilderness, Appomattox, are of more surpassing interest than the dramatic political changes,—the downfall of the Whig party, the swift rise and the equally swift submergence of the Know-Nothing party, the birth of the Republican party, the disruption and overthrow of the long-dominant Democratic party,—through which the [Pg 2] country came at last to see that only the sword could make an end of the long controversy between the North and the South.

The first years of the decade were marked by the passing of one group of statesmen and the rise of another group. Calhoun's last speech in the Senate was read at the beginning of the debate over those measures which finally took shape as the Compromise of 1850. The Compromise was the last instance of the leadership of Clay. The famous Seventh of March speech in defense of it was Webster's last notable oration. These voices stilled, many others took up the pregnant theme. Davis and Toombs and Stephens and other well-trained Southern statesmen defended slavery aggressively; Seward and Sumner and Chase insisted on a hearing for the aggressive anti-slavery sentiment; Cass and Buchanan maintained for a time their places as leaders in the school of compromise. But from the death of Clay to the presidential election of 1860 the most resonant voice of them all was the voice of Stephen Arnold Douglas. It is scarcely too much to say that [Pg 3] during the whole period the centre of the stage was his, and his the most stirring part. In 1861, the curtain fell upon him still resolute, vigorous, commanding. When it rose again for another scene, he was gone so completely that nowadays it is hard for us to understand what a place he had. Three biographers writing near the time of his death were mainly concerned to explain how he came to be first in the minds of his contemporaries. A biographer writing now must try to explain why he has been so lightly esteemed by that posterity to which they confidently committed his fame. Blind Tom, the negro mimic, having once heard him speak, was wont for many years to entertain curious audiences by reproducing those swelling tones in which he rolled out his defense of popular sovereignty, and it is not improbable that Douglas owes to the marvelous imitator of sounds a considerable part of such fame as he has among uneducated men in our time. Among historical students, however seriously his deserts are questioned, there is no question of the importance of his career.

[Pg 4]

He was born April 23, 1813, at Brandon, Vermont, the son of Stephen Arnold Douglas and Sarah Fisk, his wife. His father, a successful physician, was doubtless of Scotch descent; but the founder of the Douglas family in America was married in Northamptonshire. He landed on Cape Ann in 1639–40, but in 1660 he made his home at New London, Connecticut. Dr. Douglas's mother was an Arnold of Rhode Island, descended from that Governor Arnold who was associated with Roger Williams in the founding of the colony. Sarah Fisk's mother was also an Arnold, and of the same family. Their son was therefore of good New England stock, and amply entitled to his middle name. Dr. Douglas died suddenly of apoplexy in July, 1813; it is said that he held the infant Stephen in his arms when he was stricken. His widow made her home with a bachelor brother on a farm near Brandon, and the boy's early years were passed in an environment familiar to readers of American biography—the simplicity, the poverty, the industry, and the serious-mindedness of rural [Pg 5] New England. He was delicate, with a little bit of a body and a very large head, but quick-witted and precocious, and until he was fifteen years of age his elders permitted him to look forward to a collegiate education and a professional career.

But by that time the uncle was married, and an heir was born to him. Stephen was therefore made to understand that the expense of his education could be met only from his mother's limited means.

He promptly resolved to learn a trade, walked fourteen miles to the neighboring town of Middlebury, and apprenticed himself to a cabinet-maker. He worked at cabinet-making two years, and afterwards, even when he had risen so high that many of his countrymen were willing he should try his hand at making cabinets of men, he protested that those two years were by far the happiest of his life, and that he would never willingly have exchanged his place in the Middlebury workshop for any other place whatsoever. As it was, he left it because he was not strong enough for that sort of work.

[Pg 6]

The following year he pursued his studies at the academy of Brandon. Then his mother married again, and he went with her to the home of his stepfather, Gehazi Granger, Esquire, near Canandaigua, New York, and finished his schooling at the Canandaigua Academy, which appears to have been an excellent one. Meanwhile, he also read law, and showed great proficiency both in his classical and his legal studies. Not much is on record concerning his schoolboy life. It is known, however, that he had a way of making his fellows like him, so that they of their own accord put him forward, and that he had a lively interest in politics. It is said that even so early as the campaign of 1828, when he was but fifteen, he organized a band of his playmates to make war on the "coffin handbills" wherewith the Adams men sought to besmirch the military fame of General Jackson, already become his hero. At Canandaigua, four years later, he espoused the same cause in debating clubs, and won an ascendency among his fellows by his readiness and the extent of his information. [Pg 7] In the life of another man, these boyish performances might be set down merely as signs of promise; but Douglas was so soon immersed in real politics, and rose to distinction with such astounding swiftness, that his performances as a schoolboy may well be accounted the actual beginning, and not merely a premonition, of his career. He was only twenty, when, in June, 1833, he set forth to enter upon it.

Save that he was going West, he does not seem to have had any destination clearly in mind. He carried letters to certain persons in Cleveland, and stopped there to see them, and so made the acquaintance of Sherlock J. Andrews, a leading lawyer of the town, who persuaded him to remain and read law in his office until a year should elapse and he could be admitted to the Ohio bar. However, in less than a week he fell ill of a fever which did not leave him until the expense of it had well-nigh emptied his slender purse. His physicians, fearing he was too slight and delicate for Western hardships, urged him to go back to Canandaigua, [Pg 8] but when he left Cleveland he again turned westward, resolved in his own mind never to go back without the evidences of success in his life. It is doubtful if among all the thousands who in those days were constantly faring westward, from New England towns and the parishes of Virginia and the Carolinas, there ever was a youth more resolutely and boldly addressed to opportunity than he. Poor, broken in health, almost diminutive in physical stature, and quite unknown, he made his way first to Cincinnati, then to Louisville, then to St. Louis, in search of work. Coming almost to the end of his resources, he reasoned that it would be best for him to seek some country town, where his expenses would be slight; and guided merely by a book of travel he had read he fixed on a town which, as it happened, bore the name of his political patron saint. In November, 1833, being now twenty years and six months old, he arrived at Jacksonville, Illinois, with a sum total of thirty-seven cents in his pocket. The glimpses we get of him during his [Pg 9] wanderings, from the recollections of certain men with whom he made acquaintance in stages and on river steamboats, make a curious and striking picture of American character. The feverish, high-strung boy was never dismayed and never a dreamer, but always confident, purposeful, good-humored.

He found no work at Jacksonville, and walked to Winchester, sixteen miles to the southwestward, where he hoped to get work as a teacher. The next morning, seeing a crowd assembled in the public square of the village, he pushed his way to the centre and learned that there was to be an auction of the wares of a merchant who had recently died. The auctioneer was in need of a clerk to keep the record of the sales, and the place was offered to the young stranger. He took it, served three days, earned six dollars, made acquaintance with the farmers gathered for the sale, and got a chance in the talk about politics to display those qualities which he never failed to display when opportunity offered—the utmost readiness in debate, good-natured courtesy, and keen political [Pg 10] instinct. A school was arranged for him, and within a week he had forty pupils entered for three months. A lawyer of the place befriended him with the loan of some books, and he gave his evenings to law and politics. When the three months were ended, he went back to Jacksonville and opened an office. March 4, 1834, he was licensed to practice, and from that time he rose faster than any man in Illinois, if not in the whole country, notwithstanding that he rose on the lines along which many and many another young American was struggling toward prominence, and notwithstanding that Illinois was exceptionally full, as later years were to prove, of young men fitted for such careers as Douglas sought—notwithstanding, too, that there had already drifted to New Salem, in the very next county, a young Kentuckian destined to such eminence that the Illinois of those years is oftenest studied now for light on him, and is most amply revealed to us in the books about him.

But for the very reason that Douglas rose so fast it is not necessary, in order to understand [Pg 11] how or why he rose, to study the conditions and men he had to deal with so carefully as they have done who seek to explain for us the slower progress of that strange career with which his is indissolubly associated. Jacksonville, which was to be his home for a few years, was a small country town, but it was the county seat of Morgan, one of the two wealthiest and most populous counties in the State. A few years earlier, that whole region had been a frontier, but the first roughness was now worn away. True, the whole northern half of Illinois was practically unsettled, and Chicago was but three years old, and not yet important. But it appears that the general character of the central counties was already fixed, and what followed was of the nature of growth rather than change. Certain small towns, like Springfield, were to become cities, and certain others, like New Salem, were to disappear. Railroads were not yet, though many were planning, and manufactures were chiefly of the domestic sort. But in the matter of the opportunities it presented to aspiring youth [Pg 12] the country was already Western, and no longer wild Western. Hunting shirts and moccasins were disappearing. Knives in one's belt had gone out of fashion. The merely adventurous were passing beyond the Mississippi, and the field was open to the enterprising, the speculative, the ambitious.

Enterprise and speculation were in the air, and ambition, if it took a political turn, must perforce take account of them. The whole country was prosperous, and Illinois was possessed with the fever of development then epidemic throughout the West and the South. If one examines the legislation of any of the States west of the Alleghanies during the second administration of President Jackson, by far the most numerous category of bills will be found to deal with internal improvements, particularly railroads and canals. Money, however, was needed for these things, and Illinois, like all new countries, had to look backward to older communities for capital. President Jackson had but lately made his final assault upon the National Bank, the principal dispenser of [Pg 13] capital, by the removal of the deposits, and public opinion was much divided on his course, when Douglas opened his law office and began to discuss public questions with his neighbors. While he still lived at Winchester, he had helped to get subscribers for a Democratic newspaper at Jacksonville, and he soon called upon the editor, who was first surprised at his visitor's youthful appearance and then, as he himself tells us, at "the strength of his mind, the development of his intellect, and his comprehensive knowledge of the political history of his country."

Boy as he looked, and boy as he was, for he had not yet passed his twenty-first birthday, Douglas actually got the leadership of the Jackson party in that neighborhood before he had lived there a month. An enthusiastic supporter of the President's policy on the bank question, he talked about the matter so well on Saturdays, when, according to the Western and Southern custom, the country people flocked into town, that he was put forward to move the Jackson resolutions at a mass meeting of Democrats [Pg 14] which he and his friend, the editor, had contrived to bring about. There was a great crowd. Josiah Lamborn, an orator of some reputation, opposed the resolutions. Douglas replied in an hour's speech, discomfited Lamborn, and so swept his audience that they seized upon him and bore him on their shoulders out of the room and around the public square. He was the "Little Giant" from that day, and the speech became a Democratic tradition. Of course, in after years, the men who could say they heard it could not be expected to admit that he ever made a better speech in his life.

Within a year, he was so well known that he was chosen to the office of public prosecutor, or district attorney, of the first judicial circuit, the most important in Illinois, and his successful candidacy for the place is all the more remarkable because he was chosen by the legislature, and not by his neighbors of the circuit. Moreover, his competitor, John J. Hardin, was one of the foremost men of Illinois. It is true that Hardin was a Whig, and that by this time [Pg 15] there was a pretty clear division between Whigs and Jackson men on offices as well as measures, so that the contest was a party as well as a personal affair; but from auctioneer's clerk to district attorney was a promotion hardly to be won in a year by a youth of qualities less than extraordinary.

The election was in February, 1835, and Douglas held the office the better part of two years. A justice of the supreme court had declared, on hearing of the legislature's choice, that the stripling could not fill the place because he was no lawyer and had no law books. Nevertheless, he was an efficient prosecutor. No record of his service is available, but there was a tradition in later years that not one of his indictments was quashed. Certainly, his work in the courts of the district increased his reputation and strengthened his hold on his own party. In the spring of 1836, the Democrats of Morgan held a convention to nominate candidates for the six seats in the house of representatives to which the county was entitled. This was a novel proceeding, for the system of [Pg 16] conventions to nominate for office was not yet developed; the first of the national party conventions was held in preparation for the presidential campaign of 1832. Douglas was a leader in the movement, and as a result of it himself was drawn into the contest. Morgan was a Whig county, but the solid front of the Democracy so alarmed the Whigs that they also abandoned the old plan of letting any number of candidates take the field and united upon a ticket with Hardin at its head. No man on the Democratic ticket was a match for Hardin. One of the candidates was withdrawn, therefore, and Douglas took his place, and he and Hardin canvassed the county together in a series of joint debates. Mainly through his championship, the convention plan was approved, and the Democrats won the election; but Hardin's vote was greater than the weakest Democrat's, and so the rivalry between him and Douglas was continued in the legislature, where they took their seats in December, 1836.

In that same house of representatives were [Pg 17] John A. McClernand, James Shields, William A. Richardson, and other men who rose to national distinction. Abraham Lincoln, a Whig representative from Sangamon County, was already well known for his ungainly length of body, for his habit of reasoning in parables which were now scriptural and now vulgar to the point of obscenity, and for a quaint and rare honesty. He was four years older than the new member from Morgan, and nearly two feet taller. Douglas, many years later, declared that he was drawn to Lincoln by a strong sympathy, for they were both young men making an uphill struggle in life. Lincoln, at his first sight of Douglas, during the contest with Hardin for the attorneyship, pronounced him "the least man he ever saw."

Douglas was the youngest member of an unusual house, but he at once took his place among the leaders. When the governor's message, animadverting severely on the President's course with the Bank, brought on a discussion of national party questions, he and Hardin seem to have won the chief [Pg 18] honors of the debate. He was appointed chairman of the Committee on Petitions, to which numerous applications for divorce were referred, and introduced a resolution which passed and which put an end to divorces by act of the legislature. On the great question of the hour, the question of development and internal improvements, he declared that the State ought to attempt no improvement which it could not afford to construct and to own. He favored a few specific enterprises and the making of careful surveys and estimates before any others should be taken up. But it was the very height of "flush times" in Illinois, and the legislature added millions to the vast sums in which the State was already committed to the support of canals, railroads, river improvements, and banks. It was but a few weeks from the adjournment in March to the great financial panic of 1837, which crushed every one of the state-aided banks, stopped the railroad building and river dredging, and finally left Illinois burdened with an enormous debt. There was a special session of the legislature in the summer, [Pg 19] occasioned by the depression and hard times which had followed so hard upon the flush times of the winter, but Douglas was not there to tax his associates with their unwisdom. He had taken another step in his unexampled career of office-holding by accepting from President Van Buren the office of register of public lands at Springfield, the growing town in Sangamon County which the legislature had just made the capital of the State, and where, within a few years, Shields, McClernand, Lincoln, and other rising young men were gathered.

From this time, Douglas and Lincoln knew each other well, for they lived together several years in an atmosphere of intimate personal scrutiny. For searching study of one's fellows, for utter disregard of all superficial *criteria* of character and conventional standards of conduct, there is but one sort of life to be compared with the life of a Southern or Western town, and that is the life of students in a boarding-school or a small college. In such communities there is little division into [Pg 20] classes, as of rich and poor, educated and illiterate, well and obscurely born. On the steps of the court-house, in the post-office while the daily mail is sorted, in the corner drug store on Sundays, in lawyers' offices, on the curbstone,—wherever a group of men is assembled,—there is the freest talk on every possible subject; and the lives of men are open to their fellows as they cannot be in cities by reason of the mass or in country districts by reason of the solitude and the shyness which solitude breeds. Against Douglas there was the presumption, which every New England man who goes southward or westward has to live down, that he would in some measure hold himself aloof from his fellows. But the prejudice was quickly dispelled. No man entered more readily into close personal relations with whomsoever he encountered. In all our accounts of him he is represented as surrounded with intimates. Not without the power of impressing men with his dignity and seriousness of purpose, we nevertheless hear of him sitting on the knee of an [Pg 21] eminent judge during a recess of the court; dancing from end to end of a dinner-table with the volatile Shields—the same who won laurels in the Mexican War, a seat in the United States Senate, and the closest approach anybody ever won to victory in battle over Stonewall Jackson; and engaging, despite his height of five feet and his weight of a hundred pounds, in personal encounters with Stuart, Lincoln's athletic law partner, and a corpulent attorney named Francis.

On equal terms he mingled in good-humored rivalry with a group of uncommonly resourceful men, and he passed them all in the race for advancement. There is some reason to believe that Lincoln, strange as it seems, was his successful rival in a love affair, but otherwise Douglas left Lincoln far behind. Buoyant, good-natured, never easily abashed, his maturity and *savoir faire* were accentuated by the smallness of his stature. His blue eyes and his dark, abundant hair heightened his physical charm of boyishness; his virile movements, his face, heavy-browed, round, and strong, and his [Pg 22] well-formed, uncommonly large head gave him an aspect of intellectual power. He had a truly Napoleonic trick of attaching men to his fortunes. He was a born leader, beyond question; and he himself does not seem ever to have doubted his fitness to lead, or ever to have agonized over the choice of a path and the responsibilities of leadership. Principles he had—the principles of Jefferson and Jackson as he understood them. These, apparently, he held sufficient for every problem and every emergency of political life.

He believed in party organization quite as firmly as he believed in party principles, and in the summer of 1837 he had a hand in building up the machinery of conventions and committees through which the Illinois Democrats have governed themselves ever since. He defended Van Buren's plan of a sub-treasury when many even of those who had supported Jackson's financial measures wavered in the face of the disfavor into which hard times had brought the party in power, and in November, although the [Pg 23] Springfield congressional district, even before the panic, had shown a Whig majority of 3000, he accepted the Democratic nomination for the seat in Congress to be filled at the election in August, 1838, and threw himself with the utmost ardor into the canvass. The district was the largest in the whole country, for it included all the northern counties of the State. His opponent was John T. Stuart, Lincoln's law partner, and for five months the two spoke six days every week without covering the whole of the great region they aspired to represent. The northern counties had been filling up with immigrants, and more than 36,000 votes were cast. Many ballots were thrown out on technicalities; most of the election officials were Whigs. After weeks of uncertainty, Stuart was declared elected by a majority of five. The moral effect, however, was a triumph for Douglas, who at the time of his nomination was not of the age required of congressmen.

He announced that he would now devote himself to his profession. But it was by this [Pg 24] time very difficult, even if he so wished, to withdraw from politics. He was constantly in council with the leaders of his party, and belonged to a sort of "third house" at Springfield which nowadays would probably be called a lobby. During the winter there was an angry controversy between the Democratic governor and the Whig senate over the question of the governor's right to appoint a secretary of state, the senate refusing to confirm his nomination of McClernand on the ground that the office was not vacant. The question was brought before the supreme court, whose Whig majority, by deciding against the governor, strengthened a growing feeling of discontent with the whole judiciary among the Democrats, and Douglas took strong ground in favor of reorganizing the court. In March, addressing a great meeting at Springfield, he defended the Virginia and Kentucky resolutions of 1798, and when the presidential campaign opened in November he had a debate with Lincoln and other Whig orators. He was, in fact, the leading Democratic orator [Pg 25] throughout the campaign in Illinois, and there is no doubt that his enthusiasm and his shrewdness had much to do with the result there. Of all the Northern States, only Illinois and New Hampshire went for Van Buren.

Meanwhile, however, he had practiced law with such success that no account of the Illinois bar of those days omits his name from the list of eminent attorneys. It was noted that whereas Lincoln was never very successful save in those cases where his client's cause was just, a client with but a slender claim upon the court's favor found Douglas a far better advocate. He never seems to have given much time to the reading of law or to the ordinary drudgery of preparing cases for trial, but he mastered the main facts of his cases with the utmost facility, and his mind went at once to the points that were sure to affect the decision. Early in his experience as a lawyer he had to be content with fees that seem absurdly small; once, he rode from Springfield to Bloomington to argue a case, and got but [Pg 26] five dollars for his services. But he was a first-rate man of business, and soon had a good income from his profession.

In January, 1841, the legislature, now Democratic in both branches, removed the Whig incumbent from the office of secretary of state, and the governor at once appointed Douglas to succeed him. That office, however, he held less than a month, for the legislature had also reconstructed the supreme court in such a way as to increase the number of judges, and in February, being then less than twenty-eight years old, he was named for one of the new places. One of the reasons why the court was reconstructed was its opposition to the Democratic position on the franchise question. Douglas, arguing a famous franchise case before it, had made himself the champion of unnaturalized inhabitants claiming the right to vote, and had thus established himself in the good-will of a large and increasing constituency throughout the State. Under the new law, each justice was assigned to a particular circuit,—Douglas to the westernmost, [Pg 27] whose principal town was Quincy, on the Illinois River, where he made his home.

The Mormon settlement of Nauvoo was in that circuit, and the most interesting of all the cases brought before Judge Douglas grew out of the troubles between the followers of Joe Smith and their neighbors. On one occasion, Joe Smith was himself on trial, and the Christian populace of the neighborhood, long incensed against him and his people, broke into the court-room clamoring for his life. The sheriff, a feeble-bodied and spiritless official, showed signs of yielding, and the judge, promptly assuming a power not vested in his office, appointed a stalwart Kentuckian sheriff, and ordered him to summon a *posse* and clear the room. By these means the defendant's life was saved, and Douglas, notwithstanding various decisions of his against them, earned the gratitude of the religious enthusiasts. There is a story that some years later, when he was no longer a judge, but a major in a militia regiment sent on an expedition against Nauvoo, he was ordered to take a hundred men and arrest the "twelve [Pg 28] apostles." The Mormons, outnumbering the militia, were fortified for defense. Major Douglas, however, proceeded alone into their lines, persuaded the twelve to enter their apostolic coach and come with him to the Christian camp, and so brought about an agreement which prevented a fight.

Both as a judge and as a member of the council of revision Douglas stood out with commendable firmness against the popular feeling, strong throughout the country during the hard times, and which in some of the States got a complete ascendency over courts and legislatures, in favor of the relief of debtors. He enforced the old laws for the collection of debts, and he baulked several legislative schemes to defraud creditors of their due by declaring the new laws unconstitutional. For the rest, his decisions have seemed to competent critics to show that he possessed unusual legal ability and grasp of principles and a corresponding power of statement, scant as his legal training was.

According to the American usage, he was "Judge Douglas" all the rest of his [Pg 29] life, but the state bench no more satisfied his ambition than the other state offices he had held. In December, 1842, when the legislature proceeded to ballot for a United States senator, his name was presented, though again his age fell short of the legal requirement, and on the last ballot he had fifty-one votes against the fifty-six which elected his successful competitor. The next year, being nominated for the lower house of Congress, he accepted, and at once resigned his place on the bench, though the district had a Whig complexion. At the end of a canvass which left both himself and his opponent, Browning, seriously ill, he was elected by a majority of several hundred.

On his way to Washington, he visited Cleveland, where his westward journey had come so near an abortive ending, and then his home-folk at Canandaigua. He was but thirty years old, yet he had held five important political offices, he had risen to high rank in his profession, he was the leader of the dominant party in a great State; and all this he had done alone, unaided. Few aged [Pg 30] men have brought back such laurels from their Western fortune-seeking. In December, 1843, he took his seat in the House of Representatives and began to display before the whole country the same brilliant spectacle of daring, energy, and success which had captivated the people of Illinois.

[Pg 31]

CHAPTER II

THE HOUSE AND THE SENATE

It was the aggressive energy of the man, unrestrained by such formality as was still observed by the public men of the older Eastern communities, which most impressed those who have left on record their judgments of the young Western congressman. The aged Adams, doubtless the best representative of the older school in either branch of Congress, gave a page of his diary to one of Douglas's early speeches. "His face was convulsed,"—so the merciless diary runs,—"his gesticulation frantic, and he lashed himself into such a heat that if his body had been made of combustible matter it would have burnt out. In the midst of his roaring, to save himself from choking, he stripped and cast away his cravat, unbuttoned his waistcoat, and had the air and aspect of a half-naked pugilist. And this man comes [Pg 32] from a judicial bench, and passes for an eloquent orator!" On another occasion, the same critic tells us, Douglas "raved an hour about democracy and anglophobia and universal empire." Adams had been professor of rhetoric and oratory at Harvard College, and he was the last man in the country to appreciate an oratorical manner that departed from the established rules and traditions of the art. Ampère, a French traveler, thought Douglas a perfect representative of the energetic builders of the Western commonwealths, and predicted that he would come into power when it should be the turn of the West to dominate the country. "Small, black, stocky," so this observer described him, "his speech is full of nervous power, his action simple and strong." Douglas, however, quickly adapted himself to his new environment,—no man in the country excelled him in that art,—and took on all the polish which the Washington of that day demanded, without any loss of fighting spirit or any abandonment of his democratic manners and principles.

[Pg 33]

He soon got a good opportunity to plant himself on a powerful popular sentiment by urging, in a really excellent speech, that the country should repay to the aged Jackson the fine which had been imposed upon him for contempt of court during the defense of New

Orleans. An experienced opponent found him ready with a taking retort to every interruption. It being objected that there was absolutely no precedent for refunding the fine, "I presume," he replied, "that no case can be found on record, or traced by tradition, where a fine, imposed upon a general for saving his country, at the peril of his life and reputation, has ever been refunded." When he visited The Hermitage during the following summer, Jackson singled him out of a distinguished party and thanked him, not without reason, for defending his course at New Orleans better than he himself had ever been able to defend it. Douglas won further distinction during the session by defending, in a report from the committee on elections, the right of the several States to determine how their representatives [Pg 34] in Congress should be chosen. Later, in a debate with John J. Hardin, his rival in Congress as in the Illinois legislature, he contrasted the Whig and Democratic positions on the questions of the day with so much force and skill that the speech was used as the principal Democratic document in the presidential campaign of 1844.

In Congress, distinction does not always, or usually, imply power; but Douglas was consummately fit for the sort of struggling by which things are in fact accomplished at Washington. Whatever the matter in hand, his mind always moved with lightning rapidity to positive views. He was never without a clear purpose, and he had the skill and the temper to manage men. He knew how to conciliate opponents, to impress the thoughtful, to threaten the timid, to button-hole and flatter and cajole. He breathed freely the heated air of lobbies and committee rooms. Fast as his reputation grew, his actual importance in legislation grew faster still. At the beginning of his second term he was appointed chairman of the [Pg 35] House Committee on Territories, and so was charged in an especial way with the affairs of the remoter West. In the course of that service, he framed many laws which have affected very notably the development of our younger commonwealths. He was particularly opposed to the policy of massing the Indians in reservations west of the Mississippi, fearing that the new Northwest, the Oregon country, over which we were still in controversy with Great Britain, would thus be isolated. To prevent this, he introduced during his first term a bill to organize into a territory that part of the Louisiana Purchase which lay north and west of Missouri. As yet, however, there were scarcely any white settlers in the region, and no interest could be enlisted in support of the bill. But he renewed his motion year after year until finally, as we shall see, he made it the most celebrated measure of his time.

His advocacy of the internal improvements needed for the development of the West brought him in opposition to a powerful element in his own party. Adams, writing [Pg 36] in his diary under date of April 17, 1844, says: "The Western harbor bill was taken up, and the previous question was withdrawn for the *homunculus* Douglas to poke out a speech in favor of the constitutionality of appropriations for the improvement of Western rivers and harbors. The debate was continued between the conflicting absurdities of the Southern Democracy, which is slavery, and the Western Democracy, which is knavery." Under the leadership of Jackson and other Southerners, the Democrats, notwithstanding their long ascendency, had adhered to their position on internal improvements more consistently, perhaps, than to any other of the contentions which they had made before they came into power. Douglas did not, indeed, commit himself to that interpretation of the Constitution which justified appropriations for any enterprise which could be considered a contribution to the "general welfare," and he protested against various items in river and harbor bills. But as a rule he voted for the bills.

[Pg 37]

He was particularly interested in the scheme for building a railroad which should run north and south the entire length of Illinois, and favored a grant of public lands to aid the State in the enterprise. For years, however, he had to contend with a corporation which had got from the State a charter for such a railroad and was now trying to get help from Congress. In 1843, and for several sessions thereafter, bills were introduced to give aid directly to the Great Western Railway Company, and it was mainly the work of Douglas that finally secured a majority in Congress for the plan of granting lands to the State, and not to the company. That was in 1851. To his chagrin, however, the promoters of the company then persuaded the Illinois legislature to pass a bill transferring to them whatever lands Congress might grant to the State for the railroad. He at once sent for Holbrook, the leading man in the company, and informed him that no bill would be permitted to pass until he and his associates should first execute a release of all [Pg 38] the rights they had obtained from the legislature. Such a release they were at last forced to sign, the bill passed, and the Illinois Central was built. It became an important agency in the development, not of Illinois merely, but of the whole Mississippi Valley; and it is the most notable material result of Douglas's skill in legislation. But throughout the whole course of his service at Washington he never neglected, in his concern about the great national questions with which his name is forever associated, the material interests of the people whom he especially represented. His district and his State never had cause to complain of his devotion to his party and his country.

But the questions which had the foremost place while he was a member of the lower house were questions of our foreign relations, and as it happened they were questions to which he could give himself freely without risking his distinctive rôle as the champion of the newer West. The Oregon boundary dispute and the proposed annexation of [Pg 39] Texas were uppermost in the campaign of 1844, and on both it was competent for him to argue that an aggressive policy was demanded by Western interests and Western sentiment. It was in discussing the Oregon boundary that he first took the attitude of bitter opposition to all European, and particularly to all English interference in the affairs of the American continents which he steadily maintained thereafter. The long-standing agreement with Great Britain for joint occupation of the Oregon country he characterized as in practice an agreement for non-occupation. Arguing in favor of giving notice of the termination of the convention, he shrewdly pointed out that as the British settlers were for the most part fur-traders and the American settlements were agricultural, we would "squat them out" if no hindrance were put upon the westward movement of our pioneers. He would at once organize a territorial government for Oregon, and take measures to protect it; if Great Britain threatened war, he would put the country in a state of defense. "If [Pg 40] war comes," he cried, "let it come. We may regret the necessity which produced it, but when it does come, I would administer to our citizens Hannibal's oath of eternal enmity. I would blot out the lines on the map which now mark our territorial boundaries on this continent, and make the area of liberty as broad as the continent itself." He even broke with the Polk administration when it retreated from the advanced position which the party had taken during the campaign, and was one of a hardy ten who, in the debate over the resolutions that led to the final settlement, voted for a substitute declaration that the question was "no longer a subject of negotiation and compromise." There can be little doubt that his hostility to England, as well as his robust Americanism, commended him at that time to the mass of his countrymen everywhere but in the commercial East.

On the annexation of Texas, popular sentiment, even in his own party, was far from unanimous, but the party was, nevertheless, thoroughly committed to it. After the [Pg 41] election, when it appeared that Tyler was quite as favorable to the measure as his incoming Democratic successor, Douglas was one of those who came forward with a new plan for annexing territory by joint resolution of Congress, and in January, 1845, he stated as well as it ever has been stated the argument that Texas became ours by the Louisiana Purchase of 1803, and was without the consent of her people retroceded to Spain by the treaty of 1819. When President Polk sent in his announcement that war existed by the act of Mexico, Douglas was ready with a defense of that doubtful *casus belli* and an ardent support of the army bill which followed. His speech on the army bill was an admirable exhibition of his powers, and it was the best speech on that side in the debate. Adams, who interrupted him, was instantly put upon the defensive by a citation from the argument which he himself, as Secretary of State, had made in 1819 for the American claim to the line of the Rio del Norte. When he asked if the treaty of peace and boundaries concluded by Mexico [Pg 42] and Texas in 1836 had not since been discarded by the Mexican government, Douglas retorted that he was unaware of any treaty ever made by a Mexican government which was not either violated or repudiated. Adams came finally to acknowledge the unusual powers of the Western "*homunculus*" as a debater.

But the reputation and the influence won in the House of Representatives were to be extended in a more favorable arena. In 1846, Douglas being now thirty-three years of age, the Illinois legislature elected him United States senator for the six years beginning March 4, 1847. In April, 1847, he was married to Martha, daughter of Colonel Robert Martin, of Rockingham, N.C., a wealthy planter and a large slaveholder. Active as he continued to be in politics, he found time for business as well as love-making. He invested boldly in the lands over which Chicago was now spreading in its rapid growth and made the young city his home. His investments were fortunate, and within a few years he was a wealthy man according [Pg 43] to the standard of those times. He used his wealth freely in hospitality, in charity, and in the furtherance of his political enterprises. In the year 1856, the corner-stone of the University of Chicago was laid on land which he had given.

The assembly of which Douglas was now a member had gradually risen to a higher place in our system than the founders intended. The House, partly by reason of its exclusive right to originate measures of a certain class, partly because it was felt to be more accurately representative of the people, had at first a sort of ascendency. The great constructive measures of the first administration were House measures. Even so late as Jefferson's and Madison's administrations, one must look oftenest to the records of that chamber for the main lines of legislative history. But in Jackson's time the Senate profited by its comparative immunity from sudden political changes, by its veto on appointments, and by the greater freedom of debate which its limited membership permitted. It came to stand, as the House could [Pg 44] not, for conservatism, for deliberation, for independence of the executive. The advantage thus gained was increased as the growth of the Speaker's power into a virtual premiership and the development of the committee system undermined the importance of the individual representative, and as the more rapid increase of population in the free States destroyed in the House that balance of the sections which in the Senate was still carefully maintained. Moreover, the country no longer sent its strongest men into the White House, and the Supreme Court was no longer favorable to that theory of the government which, as Marshall expounded it, had tended so markedly to elevate the court itself. The upper house had gained not merely as against the lower, but as against the executive and the judiciary. The ablest and most experienced statesmen were apt to be senators; and the Senate was the true battleground in a contest that was beginning to dwarf all others. From the beginning to the end of Douglas's service there, saving a brief, delusive interval after the [Pg 45] Compromise of 1850, the slavery question in its territorial phase was constantly uppermost, and in the Senate, if anywhere, those measures must be devised, those compromises agreed on, which should save the country from disunion or war. There was open to him, therefore, a path to eminence which, difficult as it might prove, was at least a plain one. To win among his fellows in the Senate a leadership such as he had readily won among his fellows at school, at Jacksonville, at Springfield, in the legislature and the Democratic organization of Illinois, and such as he was rising to in the lower house when he left it, and then to find and establish the right policy with slavery, and particularly with slavery in the Territories—there lay his path. It was a task that demanded the highest powers, a public service adequate to the loftiest patriotism. How he did, in fact, attempt it, how nearly he succeeded in it, and why he failed in it, are the inquiries with which any study of his life must be chiefly concerned.

But Douglas was too alert and alive to [Pg 46] limit his share in legislation to a single subject or class of subjects. Save that he does not appear to have taken up the tariff question in any conspicuous way, he had a leading part in all the important discussions of his time, whether in the Senate or before the people. Unquestionably, his would be the best name to choose if one were attempting to throw into biographical form a political history of the period of his senatorship.

The very day he took his seat, he was appointed chairman of the Senate Committee on Territories, and so kept the rôle of sponsor for young commonwealths which he had begun to play in the House. No other public man has ever had so much to do with the organizing of Territories and the admitting of States into the Union; probably no other man ever so completely mastered all the details of such legislation. He reported the bills by which Utah, New Mexico, Washington, Kansas, Nebraska, Oregon, and Minnesota became Territories, and those by which Texas, Iowa, Florida, California, Wisconsin, Oregon, and Minnesota became States. His [Pg 47] familiarity with all questions concerning the public domain was not less remarkable. In dealing with both subjects, he seems always to have been guided by his confidence in the Western people themselves. He was for a liberal policy with individual settlers, holding that the government, in disposing of its lands, should aim at development and not at profit; and he was no less liberal in his view of the rights and privileges with which each new political community ought to be invested. As to the lands, he held to such a policy as looked forward to the time when they should be turned into farms and towns and cities. As to the government of the Territories, he held to such a policy with them as looked constantly forward to their becoming States, and his theory was that all the powers of the general government in reference to them were based on its power to admit States into the Union. To that rule of construction, however, he made a very notable exception. Declaring that the Mormons were for the most part aliens by birth, that they were trying to subvert the authority of the [Pg 48] United States, that they themselves were unfit for citizenship and their community unfit for membership in the Union, he favored the repeal of the act by which the territorial government of Utah was set up. He went farther, and maintained that only such territory as is set apart to form new States must be governed in accordance with those constitutional clauses which relate to the admission of States, and that territory acquired or held for other purposes could be governed quite without reference to any rights which through statehood, or the expectation of statehood, its inhabitants might claim. This theory of his has assumed in our later history an interest and importance far beyond any it had at the time; but Douglas in that and in many other of his speeches clearly had in mind just such exigencies as have brought us to a practical adoption of his view.

His interest in the government's efforts to develop the country, and particularly the West, by building highways, dredging rivers, and deepening harbors, did not diminish, [Pg 49] and he made more than one effort to bring design and system into that legislation. Always mindful of results, he pointed out that the conditions under which the river and harbor bills were framed,—the pressure upon every representative and senator to stand up for the interests of his constituents, and the failure to fix anywhere the responsibility for a general plan,—made it inevitable that such measures would either fail to pass or fail of their objects if they did pass. He suggested, in 1852, a plan which a year or two later, in a long letter to Governor Matteson, of Illinois, he explained and advocated with much force. It was for Congress to consent, as the Constitution provided it might, and as in particular cases it had consented, to the imposition by the States of tonnage duties, the proceeds to be used in deepening harbors. The scheme commended itself for many practical reasons; and it was more consonant with Democratic theory than the practice of direct appropriations by Congress.

However, in his ardent advocacy of a [Pg 50] Pacific railroad, Douglas made no question of the government's powers in that connection. True, in 1858, the committee of which he was a member threw the bill into the form of a mail contract in order that it might not run counter to the state-rights views of senators, but he seems to have favored every one of the numerous measures looking to the building of the road which had any prospect of success. At first, he was for three different roads, a northern, a central, and a southern, but it was soon clear that Congress would not go into the matter on so generous a scale. Arguing, then, for a central line, he used a language characteristic of his course on all questions that arose between the sections. "The North," he said, "by bending a little down South, can join it; and the South, by leaning a little to the North, can unite with it, too; and our Southern friends ought to be able to bend and lean a little, as well as to require us to bend and lean all the time, in order to join them."

His practical instinct and his democratic [Pg 51] inclinations were both apparent in the plan which he proposed in 1855 for the relief of the Supreme Court. A bill reported by the Committee on the Judiciary freed the justices from their duties on circuit and provided for eleven circuit judges. Douglas proposed, as a substitute, to divide the country into nine circuits, and to establish in each of these a court of appeals which should sit once a year and which should consist of one supreme court justice and the district judges of the circuit, the assignment of each justice to be changed from year to year. His aim was twofold: to relieve the Supreme Court by making the circuit courts the final resort in all cases below a certain importance, and to keep the justices in touch with the people, and familiar with the courts, the procedure, and the local laws in all parts of the country. The scheme, though different in details, is in its main features strikingly like the system of circuit court of appeals which was adopted in 1891.

But the questions, apart from that of slavery, on which Douglas's course has the [Pg 52] most interest for a later generation were still questions of our foreign relations. On the Clayton-Bulwer Treaty, on the Treaty of Peace with Mexico, on the Oregon Boundary Treaty of 1853, on the negotiations for the purchase of Cuba, on the filibuster expeditions of 1858, and the controversy of that year over Great Britain's reassertion of the right of search—on all these questions he had very positive opinions and maintained them vigorously. In the year 1853, he went abroad, studied the workings of European systems, and made the acquaintance of various foreign statesmen; but he did not change his opinions or his temper of mind. In England, rather than put on court costume, he gave up an opportunity to be presented to the Queen; and in Russia he appears to have made good his contention that, as persons of other nationalities are presented to foreign rulers in the dress which they would wear before their own sovereigns, an American should be presented in such dress as he would wear before the President.

But if he maintained the traditional, [Pg 53] old-fashioned American attitude toward "abroad," he was very sure, when he dealt with a particular case, to take a practical and modern line of reasoning. Opposing the treaty of peace with Mexico, he objected to the boundary line, to the promise we made never to acquire any more Mexican territory as we acquired Texas, and to the stipulations about the Indians. His objections were disregarded, and the treaty was ratified; but five years later the United States paid ten million dollars to get it altered in those respects. He vigorously opposed the Clayton-Bulwer Treaty in 1850, when it was ratified, and three years later, when the subject was brought up in open Senate, he stated at length his views on the whole subject of our relations with England and Central America, with Spain and Cuba, with European monarchies and Latin-American states. Whether right or wrong, they are the views on which the American people have acted as practical occasions have arisen and bid fair to act in the future.

It would have been possible, he thought, [Pg 54] but for Clayton's mismanagement, to get from Nicaragua a grant to the United States of exclusive and perpetual control over all railroad and canal routes through that country from the Atlantic to the Pacific. Instead, we had pledged ourselves to England "not to do, in all coming time, that which, in the progress of events, our interests, duty, and even safety may compel us to do." He opposed the treaty because it invited European intervention in American affairs; because it denied us the right to fortify any canal that might be built; because its language was equivocal in regard to the British protectorate over the Mosquito coast, and otherwise clearly contrary to the Monroe Doctrine; and because we made an unnecessary promise never to occupy any part of Central America. To all these objections, save the last, time has added force; and the principle of the last is now established in our national policy. That principle Douglas proclaimed so often that it almost rivals the principle of popular sovereignty itself in the matter of the frequency [Pg 55] of its appearance in his speeches. "You may make," he declared, "as many treaties as you please to fetter the limbs of this giant Republic, and she will burst them all from her, and her course will be onward to a limit which I will not venture to prescribe." The Alleghanies had not withheld us from the basin of the Mississippi, nor the Mississippi from the plains, nor the Rocky Mountains from the Pacific coast. Now that the Pacific barred our way to the westward, who could say that we might not turn, or ought not to turn, northward or southward? Later, he came to contemplate a time when the Pacific might cease to be a barrier: when our "interests, duty, and even safety" might impel us onward to the islands of the sea. He would make no pledges for the future. Agreements not to annex territory might be reasonable in treaties between European powers, but they were contrary to the spirit of American civilization. "Europe," he said, "is antiquated, decrepit, tottering on the verge of dissolution. When you visit her, the objects which excite your admiration are [Pg 56] the relics of past greatness: the broken columns erected to departed power. Here everything is fresh, blooming, expanding, and advancing. We wish a wise, practical policy adapted to our condition and position."

A more ardent and thoroughgoing expansionist is not to be found among eminent Americans of that time, or even of later times. While he was denouncing General Walker's lawless invasion of Central America in 1858, he took pains to make it plain that it was the filibusters' method, and not their object, which he condemned. In fact, he condemned their method chiefly because its tendency was to defeat their object.

He believed that England, notwithstanding the kinship of the two peoples and the similarity of their civilizations, was our rival by necessity, our ill-wisher because of the past. The idea that we were bound to the mother country by ties of gratitude or affection he always combated. He denied her motherhood as a historical proposition, and demanded to know of Senator Butler, of [Pg 57] South Carolina, who was moved to eloquence over America's debt to England for a language and a literature, whether he was duly grateful also for English criticism of our institutions, and particularly for the publications of English abolitionists. As to the British claim of a right to search American vessels for slaves, he was for bringing the matter at once to an issue; for denying the right *in toto*; and if Great Britain chose to treat our resistance as a cause of war, he would be for prolonging the war until the British flag should disappear forever from the American continent and the adjacent islands.

[Pg 58]

CHAPTER III

THE GREAT QUESTION

On all these questions, alike of domestic and of foreign policy, Douglas took an eminently hopeful, an eminently confident and resolute stand. His opinions were such as befitted a strong, competent, successful man. They were characteristic of the West. They were based on a positive faith in democracy, in our constitution of government, in the American people. In that faith, likewise, he addressed himself to the problem which in his day, as before and after, was perplexing the champions of democracy and giving pause to the well-wishers of the Republic. A later generation has learned to think of that problem as the negro question, a race question; Douglas's generation thought of it merely as the slavery question.

The presidential election of 1848 made a good occasion for men to take account of the [Pg 59] question, and of their own minds concerning it. In February, 1848, by the Treaty of Guadalupe Hidalgo, Mexico ceded to the United States the territory out of which California, New Mexico, and Utah have been formed. With the signing of the treaty the material elements of the problem, as it presented itself to that generation, were completely arranged.

In fifteen Southern States and in the District of Columbia slavery was sanctioned and protected by law. In fifteen Northern States slavery was prohibited by law. The foreign slave trade was long since prohibited altogether, though from time to time, in a small way, it was surreptitiously revived. The domestic slave trade, among the slave States and in the District, was still permitted. There was a law on the statute book to compel the return of slaves fleeing into the free States, but certain of its provisions had been pronounced unconstitutional, and it was ineffective. Of the territory acquired from France in 1803, all that part which lay south of the line of 36° 30′, North [Pg 60] latitude, with Missouri, which lay north of the line, was either organized into slave States or set apart for the Indians; in all that part which lay north of the line of 36° 30′, except Missouri, slavery was forbidden by a law of Congress passed in 1820. It was competent for Congress to repeal the law at any time, but from the country's long acquiescence in it, and from the circumstances of its passage, which were such that a stigma of bad faith would be fixed upon whichever section should move for its repeal, it seemed to have a force and stability more like the Constitution's itself than that of ordinary laws. There remained the territory got from Mexico, concerning which, although from the beginning of the war the question of slavery in any territory that might come to us at the end of it had been constantly in agitation, Congress had as yet passed no law. What law Congress should make about slavery in California, New Mexico, and Utah was the main question. But there was also a question of the right boundary between New Mexico and Texas, [Pg 61] which had been admitted in 1845 as a slave State, with an agreement that she might at any time divide herself up into four States.

The material elements of the problem, then, were comparatively simple, and the immediately pressing questions were easily phrased; but the intangible element of public opinion was uncommonly hard to estimate. So far as the great parties were concerned, it was impossible to fix upon either of them any general theory about slavery or any definite policy with it. Up to this time, both had apparently gone on the understanding that it was not a proper issue in political contests. A small group of unpractical men had, in fact, tried to build up a party on the issue of opposition to it, but they had no prospect of carrying a single electoral vote. The adherents of the old parties were agreed on one thing: that there was no lawful way for Congress or the people of the free States to interfere with slavery in the slave States. They were divided among themselves, inside of party lines, on the fugitive slave law, on the interstate slave trade, on slavery and the [Pg 62] slave trade in the District of Columbia, and on slavery in the Territories.

But if party lines did not yet accurately represent the divisions of opinion on these questions, there was, nevertheless, a grouping of men according to their opinions on the general question which already had its effects in politics. Every thoughtful American of that day belonged to one or another of several groups according to the view he took of two things: slavery itself, and the body of law and usage that had grown up about it. There were the abolitionists, who believed slavery to be so utterly wrong that they were ready to go all lengths to get rid of it, violating the Constitution, breaking the compromises, endangering the Union. There were the Southern fire-eaters, who not only believed slavery right but were similarly willing to go all lengths to defend and extend it. There were the moderate men who made up the bulk of the two great parties in the North, who believed slavery wrong but felt themselves bound by the compromises of the Constitution which protected [Pg 63] it where it already existed and debarred from any method of attacking it which might bring the Union into danger. There were the moderate men of the South, Whigs and Democrats alike, who believed either that slavery was right or at least that there was no better state possible for the mass of the blacks, but who were yet devoted to the Union and respected their constitutional obligations. Finally, there were men so constituted that they could decline to take any thought whether slavery were right or wrong, and could deal with every question that arose concerning it as a question of expediency merely, or of law and precedent.

To which of these groups should Douglas join himself? Up to this time, his public record was too meagre to show clearly where he stood. In 1845, when the bill to annex Texas was before the House, he had offered an amendment extending the compromise line of 1820 through the new State, so that if Texas were ever divided slavery would be prohibited in such State or States as should be formed north of that line. Both in the [Pg 64] House and in the Senate he had voted against the famous resolution of Mr. David Wilmot to exclude slavery from any territory that we might get from Mexico, and he continued to oppose that motion, in whatever form it appeared, until the legislature of Illinois instructed him to favor it. In 1848, he voted for the so-called Clayton Compromise, which proposed to organize California, Oregon, and New Mexico into Territories and merely extend over them the Constitution and laws of the United States so far as these should prove applicable; but he also voted for the bill to organize the Territory of Oregon with a clause prohibiting slavery. By his speeches, no less than by his votes, he was committed to the position that the Missouri Compromise was a final settlement so far as the Louisiana Purchase was concerned, and that the compromise line ought to be extended through the Mexican Cession to the Pacific. He was not clearly committed on any other of the points at issue between the friends and the opponents of slavery.

But he had roundly denounced the [Pg 65] abolitionists, and he had married the daughter of a slaveholder. The day after his wedding his father-in-law presented him a deed to a plantation in Mississippi and a number of slaves. He gave it back, not, so he declared, because he thought it wrong to hold slaves, but because he did not know how to govern them or to manage a plantation. His wife soon fell heir to the land and negroes, and at her death they passed to her children under a will which requested that the blacks be not sold but kept and cared for by the testator's descendants. Douglas, as the guardian of his infant children, respected their grandfather's wishes. For that reason he was called a slaveholder, and a fellow senator once openly accused him of shaping his course as a public man to accord with his private interests. He denied and disproved the charge, but proudly added: "I implore my enemies, who so ruthlessly invade the private sanctuary, to do me the favor to believe that I have no wish, no aspiration, to be considered purer or better than she who was, or they who are, slaveholders."

[Pg 66]

He was of those who could be indifferent to the moral quality of slavery. He could favor whatever policy the Constitution required, or precedents favored, or public expediency demanded; if his enemies were to be believed, he could take whatever course ambition and self-interest impelled him to. Never once during his long wrestling with the slavery question did he concede that any account should be taken of the moral character of the institution, or intimate that he believed it wrong for one man to hold another man in bondage.

The Democratic National Convention of 1848, though its platform was as vague as it could be made, nominated a candidate who was committed to a particular plan with slavery in the Territories. The candidate was Lewis Cass, of Michigan, and his plan was set forth in a letter to one Nicholson, of Nashville, Tennessee, of date December 24, 1847. The plan appeared to be a very simple one. It was to leave the people of each Territory, so soon as it should be organized, free to regulate their domestic institutions as [Pg 67] they chose. He favored it for two reasons: first, because Congress had no right to interfere; and second, because the people themselves were the best judges of what institutions they ought to have. That was the barest form of the doctrine which its opponents in derision named "squatter sovereignty." It was contrary to the doctrine of the Wilmot Proviso, which invoked the authority of Congress to exclude slavery from all the Territories, and contrary, also, to whatever doctrine or no doctrine was implied in the motion to extend the compromise line to the Pacific, exercising the authority of Congress to exclude slavery north of the line and forbearing to exercise it south of the line. It was equally contrary to a third doctrine which was brought before the convention. William L. Yancey, a delegate from Alabama, offered a resolution to the effect that neither Congress nor any territorial legislature had any right to exclude slave property from the Territories. This was a mild statement of the extreme Southern doctrine that slaves were property, so recognized by the [Pg 68] Constitution, and that a slaveholder had the right to take his slaves anywhere but into a State where slavery was forbidden.

The doctrine of Cass seemed to accord best with that democratic theory of the government which Douglas had always professed. It accorded well with his faith in the builders of the West. It alone, of all the doctrines advanced, accorded fully with his attitude of indifference to the moral quality of slavery. He soon embraced it, therefore, and for the rest of his life he was oftenest occupied embodying it in legislation, defending it, restating it to suit new conditions, modifying it to meet fresh exigencies. Cass, though his authorship of the doctrine is disputed, was at first held responsible for it, and he advocated it with great ability. But in the end men well-nigh forgot who the author of the principle was, so preëminent was Douglas as its defender. He made it his, whosesoever it was at first, and his it will always be in history.

During the session of 1848–49, he introduced a bill to admit California as a State, [Pg 69] leaving the people to settle the slavery question as they pleased. But his first great opportunity came in the session of 1849–50.

Cass had been beaten in the election. Zachary Taylor, the successful candidate of the Whigs, was a Southerner and a slaveholder, but he was elected on a non-committal platform, and he had never declared, if indeed he had ever formed, any opinions on the questions in dispute. His first message merely notified Congress that California, whither people were rushing from all parts of the country in search of gold, had of her own motion made ready for statehood; he expressed a hope that New Mexico would shortly follow her example, and recommended that both be admitted into the Union with such constitutions as they might present. Immediately, the House, where the free-soilers held a balance of power, fell into a long wrangle over the speakership; and the Senate was soon in fierce debate over certain anti-slavery resolutions presented from the legislature of Vermont. The North seemed to be united on the Wilmot Proviso as it had never before [Pg 70] been united on any measure of opposition to slavery, and the South, fearing to lose the fruits of her many victories in statesmanship, in diplomacy, and on Mexican battlefields, was threatening disunion if, by the admission of California as a free State with no slave State to balance, her equality of representation in the Senate should be destroyed. The portents were all of disagreement, struggle, disaster.

But at the end of January, Henry Clay, though he had come back to the scene of his many stirring conflicts in the past minded to be "a calm and quiet looker-on," roused himself to one more essay of that statesmanship of compromise in which he was a master. He made a plan of settlement that covered all the controversies and put it in the form of a series of resolutions. It was to admit California with her free-state constitution; to organize the remainder of the Mexican Cession into Territories, with no restriction as to slavery; to pay Texas a sum of money on condition that she yielded in the dispute over the boundary between her and [Pg 71] New Mexico; to prohibit the slave trade, but not slavery, in the District of Columbia; to leave the interstate slave trade alone; and to pass an effective fugitive slave law.

For two days, Clay spoke for his plan. Age, though it had not bereft him of his consummate skill in oratory, added pathos to his genuine fervor of patriotism as in that profound crisis of our affairs he pleaded with his fellow senators and with his divided countrymen. There followed the most notable series of set speeches in the history of Congress. One after another, the old leaders, Calhoun,

Webster, Benton, Cass, and the rest,—for all were still there,—rose and solemnly addressed themselves to the state of the country and the plan of settlement. All but Calhoun: now very near his end, he was too weak to stand or speak, and Mason, of Virginia, read for him, while he sat gloomily silent, his last bitter arraignment of the North. He was against the plan. Benton, though on opposite grounds, also found fault with it. Webster, to the rage and sorrow of his own New England, [Pg 72] gave it his support. Then the new men spoke. Jefferson Davis, on whom, as Calhoun was borne away to his grave, the mantle of his leadership seemed visibly to fall, steadfastly asserted the Southern claim that slaveholders had a right to go into any Territory with their slaves, but offered, as the extreme concession of the South, to extend the Missouri line to the Pacific if property in slaves were protected below the line. Chase, of Ohio, impressive in appearance but stiff in manner, argued weightily for the constitutionality and rightfulness of the Wilmot Proviso. Seward, of New York, though the shrewdest politician of the anti-slavery forces, enraged the Southerners and startled the country with the announcement that "a higher law than the Constitution" enjoined upon Congress to guard these fresh lands for freedom.

But none of the new men, and none of the old leaders but Clay himself, had such a part as Douglas in the actual settlement. He supported the resolutions, and as chairman of the Committee on Territories he [Pg 73] wrote and introduced two bills: one to admit California, and one to organize the Territories of New Mexico and Utah with no restrictions as to slavery and to adjust the dispute with Texas. When Clay was put at the head of a Committee of Thirteen, to which all the subjects of dispute were referred, he was often in consultation with the chairman of the Committee on Territories. Douglas was of opinion that the various measures proposed would have a better chance of passing separately than all in one, but Clay decided to deal with California, the Territories, and the Texas boundary in a single measure. This, with separate bills on the fugitive slave law and the slave trade in the District, he reported early in May. The Omnibus, as the first bill was called, was simply Douglas's two bills joined together with a wafer: the words, "Mr. Clay, from the Committee of Thirteen," were substituted for the words, "Mr. Douglas, from the Committee on Territories." But there was one important change. Douglas's bill gave the territorial legislatures authority over all [Pg 74] rightful subjects of legislation, subject to the Constitution, save that they could pass no law interfering with the primary disposal of the soil. Clay's committee, contrary to his wish, added the clause, "nor in respect to African slavery." Douglas moved to strike out the exception. He was voted down, but bided his time, persuaded another senator to renew the motion at a favorable moment, and it passed.

But the Omnibus could not pass. The death of President Taylor, who would probably have vetoed it, brought Fillmore, a friend of the compromise, into the White House; but there were only a handful of senators who favored every one of the measures so combined. Late in July, after months of debate and negotiation had wearied Clay out and driven him from the scene, all but the part relating to Utah was stricken out, and with that single passenger the Omnibus went through the Senate. Then separately, one after another, as Douglas had advised, the other measures were passed. The House quickly accepted them, Fillmore [Pg 75] signed them, and the last of the compromises was complete. Jefferson Davis had opposed it, and had often been pitted against Douglas in debate, for they were champions of contrary theories, but at the end he declared: "If any man has a right to be proud of the success of these measures, it is the senator from Illinois." The enterprise, indeed, was Clay's; his was the idea, the initiative, the general plan. It is rightly called Clay's compromise. But the execution of the plan was quite as much Douglas's work as his. When Clay died, no one had a better right than Douglas to inherit his place as the statesman and orator of compromise and conciliation.

In the defense of the settlement he was no less conspicuous. Though in the South such extremists as Yancey and Quitman declared that the so-called compromise was in fact a surrender of Southern rights and a sufficient reason for abandoning the Union, there were Northern men quite as violently exercised over what seemed to them a base truckling to the slave power. The legislature [Pg 76] of Illinois had formally instructed her senators to support the Wilmot Proviso, and Douglas had thus been compelled, all through the session, to vote for motion after motion to prohibit slavery outright in the Territories. At the end of the session, when he returned to his home, he found Chicago wrought up to a furor of protest. The city council actually voted to release officials from all obligation to enforce the fugitive slave law and citizens from all obligation to respect it. A mass meeting was about to pass resolutions approving this extraordinary action of the council and denouncing as traitors the senators and representatives who had voted for the law, when Douglas walked upon the stand, announced that the next evening he would publicly defend the measures of compromise, and demanded to be heard before he was condemned. A great audience, the greatest ever assembled in the city, listened to his defense. It was bold, skilful, successful. He avowed his authorship of three of the compromise measures, his approval of the others. He took them up one [Pg 77] by one, explained them, called for objections, and answered every objection effectively. At the end, he proposed and carried resolutions pledging the meeting to stand by the Constitution and the laws, and the meeting voted further, with but eight or ten nays, to repudiate the resolutions of the council. The next night, the council met and repealed them.

It seemed, in fact, that in planting himself on the compromise Douglas had rightly forecast the verdict of the country as a whole. An adjourned meeting of a Southern convention which had been called before the settlement with a view to some united and vigorous action took now a tone so mild that it allayed, instead of exciting, the fears of patriots. Jefferson Davis, an opponent, and Foote, a supporter of the settlement, went before the people of Mississippi as rival candidates for the governorship, and Davis was beaten. Yancey in Alabama was overthrown in his own party. Only South Carolina would not be reconciled. Throughout the North, and particularly in New England, attempts to [Pg 78] resist the fugitive slave law were sometimes violent and occasionally successful, and Charles Sumner, from Massachusetts, and Wade, from Ohio, were sent to join Seward and Chase and Hale, the aggressive anti-slavery men in the Senate. With Sumner, whose first important speech was an attack upon the law, Douglas instantly engaged in the first of many bitter controversies. An attack on a law so clearly demanded by the Constitution was, he declared, an attack on the Constitution itself, such as no senator could make without breaking his oath of office. But in little more than a year the lower House of Congress voted by a good majority that the compromise measures should be regarded as a permanent settlement. In 1852, the Democrats, assembled in national conventions at Baltimore, indorsed them in their platform. So did the Whigs; and Rufus Choate, their convention orator, was excusable for his hyperbole when he described "with what instantaneous and mighty charm they calmed the madness and anxiety of the hour."

[Pg 79]

Cass, in his seventieth year, was the leading candidate before the Democratic convention; so far as the leadership of parties can be determined in America, he was still the leader of the party. But Douglas, in his fortieth year, was pressing to the front. In the preliminary campaign he was put forward as the candidate of young America, and other State conventions than that of Illinois commended him. At Baltimore, his supporters were enthusiastic, aggressive, boisterous. His name in the long list of candidates always aroused an applause which showed that he was classed with Cass and Buchanan in the popular estimation, and not with the lesser men. Beginning with twenty votes on the first ballot, he rose steadily until on the thirty-first he led with ninety-two. But neither he nor Cass had a good following from the South. An expediency candidate, acceptable to the South, was found in Franklin Pierce, who had fought in the war with Mexico. Against him the Whigs pitted the commander-in-chief in the war. But Scott was thought to be tainted with free-soil [Pg 80] opinions. The Democrats, more thoroughly united, swept the country, and the new administration came into power with a great majority in both houses of Congress.

In neither branch of that Democratic Congress was there another man so fit to take the lead as Douglas. A new senator, coming to Washington in 1852, found him already risen to the first importance there. "His power as a debater," said this observer, "seemed to me unequaled in the Senate. He was industrious, energetic, bold, and skillful in the management of the affairs of his party. He was the acknowledged leader of the Democratic party in the Senate." It should be added that he never lost touch with the lower House. Neither was he unmindful of the President's part in making laws, but no President could be less disposed than Pierce was to set up his will against any measure which might come to him stamped with the party stamp. Douglas's wife died early in 1853, and in the summer he made his journey to Europe. When he returned, he was in a position the most [Pg 81] favorable for original and constructive statesmanship. By virtue of his leadership of the Senate, he was in effect the leader of Congress. He had the power of initiative. He was at the age when men are ripest for enterprises of pith and moment. Unhesitatingly, he advanced to the front and centre of the stage. When the session ended, his name was forever associated with a law that upset precedents and traditions, divided old parties and summoned up new ones, made—and unmade—history.

January 4, 1854, Mr. Douglas, from the Committee on Territories, reported a bill to form the Territory of Nebraska out of that part of the Louisiana Purchase which lay west and north of Missouri.

[Pg 82]

CHAPTER IV

LEADERSHIP

There was nothing new in the main proposal. A bill to organize this same Territory had passed the House the year before. It was generally conceded that the region ought to have a territorial government. Vast as it was, it had less than a thousand white inhabitants, but the overland route to the Pacific ran across it, and there was sure to be a rapid immigration into it so soon as it should be thrown open to settlers. What was both new and startling was a clause permitting the inhabitants of the Territory, whenever it should be admitted to statehood, to decide for themselves whether they would have slavery or not. The eighth section of the Compromise Act of 1820 provided that slavery should never exist anywhere in the Louisiana Purchase north [Pg 83] of 36° 30´, North latitude, save in the State of Missouri.

In the report which accompanied the bill, Douglas declared that it was based on the principles of the compromise measures of 1850. Those measures, he maintained, affirmed three propositions: questions relating to slavery in the Territories and in States to be formed out of them should be left to the people thereof; cases involving title to slaves and questions of personal freedom should be left to the local courts, with a right of appeal to the Supreme Court of the United States; the mandate of the Constitution concerning fugitive slaves applied to Territories as well as States. Three days later, these propositions were incorporated in the bill.

January 16, Archibald Dixon, a senator from Kentucky, offered an amendment expressly repealing the eighth section of the Missouri Compromise law. Douglas remonstrated, but in a few days he called on Dixon, the two senators went for a drive, and in the course of it Douglas promised to accept the amendment. He was satisfied, so Dixon [Pg 84] reported his conversation, that the Missouri Compromise was unconstitutional and that it was unfair to the South. "This proceeding," he said, "may end my political career, but, acting under the sense of duty which animates me, I am prepared to make the sacrifice. I will do it." January 22, with several other congressmen, he called on Jefferson Davis, Secretary of War, and was by him conducted to the White House. Contrary to his usage, for it was Sunday, the President granted them an interview. At the end of it, he promised to support the repeal. The next day, Douglas reported a substitute for the Nebraska bill. It provided for two Territories, Kansas and Nebraska, instead of one; and it declared the eighth section of the Missouri Compromise law to be inoperative because it was "superseded by" the principles of the compromise of 1850.

At the report and the bill in its first form the anti-slavery men in Congress took instant alarm. By the time the substitute was presented, the whole country knew that [Pg 85] something extraordinary was afoot. Without a sign of any popular demand, without preliminary agitation or debate, Douglas, of Illinois, had set himself to repeal the Missouri Compromise. He had undertaken to throw open to slavery a great region long consecrated to freedom. He had written the bill of his own motion, by himself, in his own house. The South had not asked for the concession, the North had not in any wise consented to it. For a little while, in fact, the Southern leaders seemed to distrust the bill, for they distrusted Douglas; one or two of them, like Sam Houston, of Texas, resisted it to the last, declaring it was sure in the end to do the South more harm than good. But for the most part they came quickly into line behind Douglas, though they never generally accepted his principle of popular sovereignty. As to the North, the challenge of the Kansas-Nebraska bill met there with such a response as no Southern aggression had yet provoked. Through every avenue of expression—through the press and the pulpit, in petitions to Congress, [Pg 86] in angry protests of public meetings and solemn resolves of legislatures—a hostile and outraged public opinion broke upon Douglas and his bill. His own party could not be held in line. Scores of Democratic newspapers turned against him. Save the legislature of Illinois, no Northern assembly, representative or other, that could speak with any show of authority, dared to support him. No Southern fire-eater was ever half so reviled. He could have traveled from Boston to Chicago, so he afterwards declared, by the light of his own burning effigies.

But the firmest and clearest protest of all came from the sturdy little band of anti-slavery men in Congress. The day after Douglas proposed his substitute, it came up for debate, and Chase, of Ohio, speaking for the opposition, asked for more time to examine the new provisions. Douglas granted a week, and the next day there appeared in various newspapers an address to the country entitled "An Appeal of the Independent Democrats in Congress." Chase was the principal author of it; he and Sumner and [Pg 87] four representatives signed it. They denounced the bill as a breach of faith, infringing the historical compact of 1820, and as part of a plot to extend the area of slavery; and they accused Douglas of hazarding the dearest interests of the American people in a presidential game.

That judgment of him and of the bill was probably accepted by a majority of his contemporaries. For lack of Southern support, he had missed the Democratic nomination in 1852. It seemed clear that whatever Northern candidate the South should prefer would be nominated in 1856. His rivals were all, in one way or another, commending themselves to the South. Pierce was hand in glove with Davis and other Southern leaders. Marcy, in the Department of State, and Buchanan, in a foreign mission, were both working for the annexation of Cuba, a favorite Southern measure. It was suspected that Cass, old as he was, had it in mind to move the repeal when Douglas went ahead of him.

The contemporaries of Douglas were under a necessity to judge his motives, for they [Pg 88] had to pass upon his fitness for high office and great responsibilities, and no other motive than ambition was so natural and obvious an explanation of his course. But it is questionable if any such positive judgment as was necessary, and therefore right, in his contemporaries, is obligatory upon historians. What he did was in accord with a political principle which he had avowed, and it was not in conflict with any moral principle he had ever avowed, for he did not pretend to believe that slavery was wrong. True, he had once thought the Missouri Compromise a sacred compact; but there were signs that he had abandoned that opinion. It is enough to decide that he took a wrong course, and to point out how ambition may very well have led him into it. It is too much to say he knew it was wrong, and took it solely because he was ambitious.

But if he had taken a wrong course he did not fail to do that which will often force us, in spite of ourselves, into admiration for a man in the wrong: he pursued it unwavering to the end. Neither the swelling uproar [Pg 89] from without nor a resolute and conspicuously able opposition within the Senate daunted him for a moment. He pressed the bill to its passage with furious energy. He set upon Chase savagely, charging him with bad faith in that he had gained time, by a false pretense of ignorance of the bill, to flood the country with slanderous attacks upon it and upon its author. The audacity of the announcement that the Compromise of 1850 repealed the Compromise of 1820 was well-nigh justified by the skill of his contention. It was a principle, he maintained, and no mere temporary expedient, for which Clay and Webster had striven, which both parties had indorsed, which the country had acquiesced in,—the principle of "popular sovereignty." That principle lay at the base of our institutions; it was illustrated in all the achievements of our past; it, and it alone, would enable us in safety to go on and extend our institutions into new regions. Cass, though he made difficulties about details, supported the bill, and the Southerners played their part well. But [Pg 90] Douglas afterwards said, and truly: "I passed the Kansas-Nebraska act myself. I had the authority and power of a dictator throughout the whole controversy in both houses. The speeches were nothing. It was the marshaling and directing of men and guarding from attacks and with ceaseless vigilance preventing surprise."

Chase was the true leader of the opposition, and he was equipped with a most thorough mastery of the slavery question in its historical and constitutional aspects. By shrewd amendments he sought to bring out the division between the Northern and Southern supporters of the bill; for the Southerners held that slave-owners had a constitutional right to go into any Territory with their property,—a right with which neither Congress nor a territorial legislature could interfere. Douglas, however, managed to avoid the danger. He made another change in the important clause. To please Cass and others, he made it declare that the Compromise of 1820 was "inconsistent with" instead of "superseded by" the principles [Pg 91] of the later compromise; and then he added the words, "it being the true intent and meaning of this act not to legislate slavery into any Territory or State, nor to exclude it therefrom, but to leave the inhabitants thereof perfectly free to form and regulate their domestic institutions in their own way, subject only to the Constitution of the

United States." That, as Benton said, was a little stump speech incorporated in the bill; and it proved a very effective stump speech indeed.

Neither the logic and the accurate knowledge of Chase, nor the lofty invective of Sumner, nor the smooth eloquence of Everett, nor Seward's rare combination of political adroitness with an alertness to moral forces, matched, in hand to hand debate, the keen-mindedness, the marvelous readiness, and the headlong force of Douglas. Their set speeches were impressive, but in the quick fire, the question-and-answer, the give-and-take of a free discussion, he was the master of them all. When, half an hour after midnight of the third of March, he rose before [Pg 92] a full Senate and crowded galleries to close the debate, he was at his best. Often interrupted, he welcomed every interruption with courtesy, and never once failed to put his assailant on the defensive. Now Sumner and now Chase was denying that he had come into office by a sacrifice of principle; now Seward was defending his own State of New York against a charge of infidelity to the compact of 1820; now Everett, friend and biographer and successor of Webster, was protesting that he had not meant to misrepresent Webster's views. Always, after these encounters, Douglas knew how to come back, with a graver tone, to the larger issue, as if they, and not he, were trying to obscure it. A spectator might have fancied that these high-minded men were culprits, and he their inquisitor. Now and then, as when he dealt with the abolitionists, there was no questioning the sincerity of his feeling, and it stirred him to a genuine eloquence. He was not surprised that Boston burned him in effigy. Had not Boston closed her Faneuil Hall upon the aged Webster? Did not [Pg 93] Sumner live there? And he turned upon the senator from Massachusetts: "Sir, you will remember that when you came into the Senate, and sought an opportunity to put forth your abolition incendiarism, you appealed to our sense of justice by the sentiment, 'Strike, but hear me first!' But when Mr. Webster went back in 1850 to speak to his constituents in his own self-defense, to tell the truth and to expose his slanderers, you would not hear him, but *you struck him first.*" Again and again, as at the end of a paragraph of unadorned but trenchant sentences the small, firm-knit figure quivered with a leonine energy, the great, swart head was thrown backward, and the deep voice swelled into a tone of triumph or defiance, the listeners could not forbear to applaud. Once, even Seward broke forth: "I have never had so much respect for him as I have to-night."

The vote in the Senate was 27 ayes to 14 noes; but in the House the opposition was dangerously strong, and but for the precaution of securing the support of the administration [Pg 94] the bill might have failed. There was a fierce parliamentary battle. Richardson, Douglas's friend and chief lieutenant, kept the House in continuous session thirty-six hours trying to force through a motion to fix a term for the debate. Feeling rose on both sides. Personal encounters were imminent. Douglas, in constant attendance, watched every move of the opposition and was instant with the counter-move. It was a month before the bill could be brought to a vote, and then it passed, with a slight change, by a majority of thirteen. At the end of May, the President signed it, and Douglas, turning from the work of enacting it into law to the harder task of defending it before the country, beheld the whole field of national politics transformed. The Whig party, crushed to earth in 1852, made no move to take a stand on the new issue; it was dead. His own historical Democratic party was everywhere throughout the North in a turmoil that seemed to forebode dissolution. One new party, sprung swiftly and secretly into life on the old issue of enmity [Pg 95] to foreigners and Roman Catholics, seemed to stand for the idea that the best way to meet the slavery issue was to run away from it. Another new party, conceived in the spirit of the appeal of the independent Democrats, was struggling to be born. State after State was falling under the power of the Know-Nothings; and those men, Whigs and Democrats alike, who for years had been awaiting an opportunity to fight slavery outside of its breastworks of compromise, were forming at last under the name of Anti-Nebraska men. Before long, they began to call themselves Republicans.

He did not quail. Invited to pronounce the Independence Day oration at Philadelphia, he made of it the first thoroughgoing denunciation of the Know-Nothings that any eminent public man in the country had the courage to make. Democrats everywhere, bewildered by the mystery in which these new adversaries shrouded their designs, were heartened to an aggressive warfare. Some months later, he took the stump in Virginia, where Henry A. Wise had brought the [Pg 96] Democrats firmly into line against the only rivals they had in the South, now that the Whigs were giving up the fight. The campaign was a crucial one, and the Know-Nothings never recovered from their defeat. Douglas's course had the merit of consistency as well as courage, for he had always championed the rights of the foreign born.

The Independence Day oration was also his first popular defense of the Kansas-Nebraska bill. But so soon as Congress adjourned he hastened home to face his own people of Illinois. Chicago was once more, as in 1850, a centre of hostility, and he announced that he would speak there the evening of September first. When the time came, flags at half mast and the dismal tolling of church bells welcomed him. A vast and ominously silent crowd was gathered, but not to hear him. Hisses and groans broke in upon his opening sentences. Hour after hour, from eight o'clock until midnight, he stood before them; time and again, as the uproar lessened, his voice combated it; but they would not let him speak. [Pg 97] Nothing, in fact, but his resolute bearing saved him from violence. On the way home, his carriage was set upon and he was in danger of his life.

Wherever he went in Northern Illinois, similar scenes were enacted. But he got a hearing, and in the central counties and in "Egypt," the southern part of the State, where the people were largely of Virginian and Kentuckian descent, he was cordially received. He kept his hold upon his party in Illinois, and Illinois, alone of all the Northwestern States, would not go over completely to the opposition. The Democratic candidate for state treasurer was elected. The Know-Nothings and Anti-Nebraska men got a majority of the congressmen, and by the defection of certain state senators who held over from a previous election they were enabled to send Lyman Trumbull, Anti-Nebraska Democrat, to be Douglas's colleague at Washington. That, when compared with the results elsewhere in the North, was a striking proof of Douglas's power with his people. Moreover, the Democrats of the [Pg 98] North who remained in the party had accepted his leadership. In the South, the party organization was soon free of any effective opposition. The two wings, so long as they were united, could still control the Senate and elect presidents. All would still be well, if only all went well on those

Western plains whither Douglas declared that the slavery question was now banished forever from the halls of Congress.

But all was not going well there. When the Kansas-Nebraska bill passed, Sumner exultantly exclaimed: "It sets freedom and slavery face to face, and bids them grapple." Nebraska was conceded to freedom, but the day Kansas, the southern Territory, was thrown open to settlement, a long, confused, confusing struggle began. The whole country was drawn into it. Blue lodges in the South, emigrant aid societies in the North, hurried opposing forces into the field. The Southerners, aided by colonized voters from Missouri, got control of the territorial legislature and passed a slave code. The Free-Soilers, ignoring the government thus established, [Pg 99] gathered in convention at Topeka, formed a free state constitution, and demanded to be admitted into the Union as a State. When a new Congress assembled in December, 1855, there were two governments in Kansas, and the people were separated into hostile camps. Brawls were frequent, and it was clear that very soon, unless the general government intervened, there would be concerted violence. A force of several thousand pro-slavery men, encamped on the Wakarusa River, were threatening Lawrence, the principal Free-Soil town. The Free-Soil men were in a majority, but their course had been in disregard of law. The pro-slavery men were in a minority, they had resorted to violence and fraud, but they had followed the forms of law.

President Pierce, swayed by Jefferson Davis, took the side of slavery. The House was nearly two months organizing, and then the President sent in a message to Congress denouncing the Free-Soilers for resisting the laws. He followed it up with a proclamation, and placed United States troops at the disposal [Pg 100] of the regular territorial government. In March, Douglas, from his Committee on Territories, made a long report on all that had occurred. He, too, laid the blame on the emigrant aid societies. He was against the Topeka constitution, and offered, instead, a bill providing for the admission of Kansas, so soon as her population should reach 93,000, which would entitle her to one representative in Congress, with such constitution as her people might lawfully adopt. The House, with an anti-slavery majority, was for admitting Kansas at once with the Topeka constitution. So was the anti-slavery group in the

Senate, now swelled into a strong minority. In the fierce debate that followed, Douglas had to defend the results, as well as the theory, of his law. Sumner was the bitterest of his assailants, and their controversy passed all bounds of parliamentary restraint. In Sumner's famous speech on the crime against Kansas, Butler, of South Carolina, was represented as the Don Quixote of slavery, Douglas as its Sancho Panza, "ready to do all its humiliating offices." The day [Pg 101] after that speech, Lawrence was sacked, and civil war broke out in Kansas. The next day, Preston Brooks, of South Carolina, assaulted Sumner and beat him down on the floor of the Senate. Ten days later, the Democratic convention met at Cincinnati to name a candidate for the presidency.

Douglas had won a good following from the South, but Pierce was the first choice of the Southerners. They wanted a servant merely, not a leader, in the White House. But it was no longer a question of the South's preference alone: it was a question of holding the two or three Northern States that were still Democratic. Of these, Pennsylvania was the most important. Buchanan was the choice of the Northern delegates because he was a Pennsylvanian and because, abroad on a foreign mission, he had escaped all responsibility for Kansas. On the first ballot, he led with 135 votes, Pierce was second with 122, and Douglas had but 33, but as before he rose as the balloting proceeded. Pierce's vote fell away; after the fourteenth ballot, his name was withdrawn. On the [Pg 102] fifteenth, Buchanan had 168, Douglas 118. Richardson, Douglas's manager, thereupon arose and read a dispatch from his chief directing his friends to obey the will of the majority and give Buchanan the necessary two thirds. Once more, the prize escaped him, though he had bid for it with his country's peace.

But the platform proclaimed the principle of his famous law to be "the only sound and safe solution of the slavery question." He was at the head of his party as Clay had for so many years headed the Whigs. He had the substance of power, the reality of leadership, whosesoever the trappings and the title might be. Every move in Congress was made with a view to its effect in the campaign, and it was he who arranged the issues. Toombs, of Georgia, offered an enabling act of admirable fairness, intended to secure the people of Kansas in their right to have such a state constitution as they might prefer, and Douglas adopted it and held the Senate for it against the House bill to admit Kansas with the Topeka constitution. [Pg 103] No agreement could be reached, for the Republicans in their platform had declared for the prohibition of slavery in all the Territories. "Bleeding Kansas" was their war-cry, and Douglas charged, not without reason, that they meant to keep Kansas bleeding until the election. The House went so far as to attach a rider to the army appropriation bill forbidding the President to employ United States troops in aid of the territorial authorities, and would not permit the appropriations to pass in their ordinary form until Congress adjourned and the President was forced to call an extra session.

But the Republican party had not yet gathered into its ranks all those who in their hearts favored its policy. The reality of civil war in Kansas brought a sobering sense of danger to the Union which worked contrary to the angry revolt against the slave power, and Buchanan's appeal to the lovers of the Union in both sections was successful. He was elected, and the Democrats, with a majority in both houses of Congress, got [Pg 104] once more a free hand with Kansas and the slavery question.

They had, too, a majority of the Supreme Court, and now for the first time the court came forward with its view of the question. Two days after the inauguration, the Dred Scott decision was handed down, and the territorial controversy passed into a new phase. All parties were forced to reconsider their positions. Douglas, especially, had need of all his adroitness to bring his doctrine of popular sovereignty into accord with the decision; for so far as it went it accorded completely with that extreme Southern view of Calhoun's and Yancey's and Jefferson Davis's which he had never yet, in his striving after an approachment with the South, ventured far enough to accept. The court decided that the Declaration of Independence did not mean negroes when it declared all men to be equal; that no negro could become a citizen of the United States; that the right of property in slaves was affirmed in the Constitution; and that Congress had no power to prohibit slavery in [Pg 105] any Territory. The announcement that the eighth clause of the Missouri Compromise law was unconstitutional was acceptable enough to the man who had accomplished its repeal, but what became of popular sovereignty if the Constitution itself decreed slavery into the Territories? But Douglas, whether he met the difficulty effectively or not, faced it promptly. Speaking at Springfield in June, he indorsed the decision, not merely as authoritative, but as right; and he claimed that it was in accord with his doctrine. For slavery, he pointed out, was dependent for its existence anywhere upon positive legislation. This the inhabitants of a Territory, acting through their territorial legislature, could grant or deny as they chose. The constitutional right of a slaveholder to take his property into a Territory would avail him nothing if he found there no laws and police regulations to protect it.

The decision was, however, universally and rightly considered a great victory for slavery. It condemned the Republican programme as unconstitutional, and it strengthened [Pg 106] the contention of the Southerners. But the Southern leaders were in little need of heartening: no cause ever had bolder and firmer champions. Under cover of the panic of 1857, which drew men's minds away from politics, a group of them were already planning a most daring last attempt to bring Kansas into the Union as a slave State. In the grappling there, freedom had shown itself stronger than slavery. Robert J. Walker, a slaveholder, whom Buchanan and Douglas had persuaded to accept the governorship, reported that the Free-Soilers outnumbered their adversaries three to one. The legislature had provided for the election of delegates to a constitutional convention, and when the question of submitting the constitution to the people arose, the governor, an upright man, promptly announced that it would be submitted, and the administration sustained him. Many Free-Soilers, however, made the mistake of staying away from the polls on election day. The convention, under control of the pro-slavery leaders, met in October at Lecompton, drew up a [Pg 107] constitution which safeguarded slavery elaborately, and hit upon an extraordinary way to submit it to the people. The electors were permitted to vote either "for the constitution with slavery," or "for the constitution without slavery," but not against the constitution as a whole. Even if "the constitution without slavery" carried, such slaves as were already held in Kansas could continue to be held.

So far had the Democratic party progressed toward the extreme Southern view, and such was the ascendency of the Southerners over Buchanan, that he would not stand up against the outrageous scheme, and it seemed on the point of succeeding. But Douglas was come now to a parting of the ways. Forced to choose between absolute subserviency to the South and what was left of his principle of popular sovereignty, he remonstrated angrily with the President for breaking faith with Walker and the Kansans. At the end of a stormy interview, Buchanan, stirred out of his wonted placidity, threateningly reminded the senator that [Pg 108] no Democrat ever broke with a Democratic administration without being crushed. Douglas scornfully retorted: "Mr. President, I wish you to remember that General Jackson is dead." The new Congress was no sooner assembled than the Lecompton programme became the central issue, and Douglas, in flat rebellion against his party's Southern masters, in open defiance of his party's President, was again the man of the hour.

Superb fighter that he was, he had a fighter's best opportunity,— great odds to fight against, and at last a good cause to fight for. The administration proscribed him. The whole South, so lately reciting his praises, rose up against him and reviled him as a traitor. Of his party associates in the Senate, but two or three were brave enough to follow him. Moreover, the panic had swept away his wealth. He was near the end of his term of office, and the trend in Illinois was toward the Republicans. The long tide which had so steadily borne him on to fortune seemed to ebb. Married again but recently, and to the most beautiful woman [Pg 109] in Washington, he must have had in mind, as he took up his new rôle, some such thought as that which fortified his favorite hero at Marengo: one battle was lost, but there was time enough to win another.

The Lecompton plotters had reckoned on the opposition of the Republicans. It was Douglas and his handful of followers who confounded them. At once, they accused him of deserting them to make sure of his reëlection to the Senate. But as the debate progressed, and his name kept appearing on the same side with Sumner's and Seward's in the divisions, another notion spread. Horace Greeley and other Republicans began to suggest that he might be the man to lead the new party to victory on a more moderate platform. Throughout the North, people who had abhorred him came first to wonder at him and then to praise him.

But he fought the Lecompton conspiracy from his old base. It was contrary to the principle of the Kansas-Nebraska Act; there had been gross frauds at the election of [Pg 110] delegates; the form of submission was a mockery of the electors. He would say nothing for slavery or against it. He cared not "whether slavery was voted up or voted down." Give the people a fair and free chance to form and adopt a constitution, and he would accept it. Let them have a fair vote on the Lecompton constitution, and if they ratified it he would accept that. Ratified it was at the absurd election the convention had ordered, for the great majority of the settlers could not vote their opposition, but when the legislature, now Free-Soil, took the authority to submit it as a whole, the majority against it by far exceeded the highest total of votes the pro-slavery men had ever mustered. Nevertheless, the Senate passed it, Douglas and three other Democrats voting in the negative. His following in the House was greater, and the bill was there amended so as to provide for submitting the constitution to the people. There was a conference, and in its final form the bill offered the people of Kansas a bribe of lands if they would accept the constitution, [Pg 111] and threatened them with an indefinite delay of statehood if they should reject it. Douglas, however, after some hesitation, refused to vote for the bill as amended, and when the time came the Kansans, by more than five to one, rejected the constitution and the bribe.

So the session brought no settlement, and Kansas was still the burning issue when Douglas went back to Illinois and took the stump in the senatorial campaign. Victor in a stirring parliamentary contest, this time Chicago welcomed him. But there awaited him treason in the ranks of his own party,—for the administration, beaten in Congress, attacked him at home,—and an opposition now completely formed and led by a man whom Douglas himself, in his own heart, dreaded as he had never dreaded the ablest of his rivals at Washington. The Republicans had taken the unusual course of holding a convention to nominate their candidate for the Senate, and the candidate was Abraham Lincoln.

[Pg 112]

CHAPTER V

THE RIVALS

Hamilton and Jefferson, Clay and Jackson, Douglas and Lincoln,—these are the three great rivalries of American politics. The third was not the least. If it fell short of the others in variety of confrontments, if it was not so long drawn out, or accompanied with so frequent and imposing alignments and realignments of vast contending forces on a broad and national field, it surpassed them in the clearness of the sole and vital issue it involved, in a closer contact and measuring of powers, in the complete and subtle correspondence of the characters of the rivals to the causes for which they fought.

Douglas was the very type of that instant success which waits on ability undistracted by doubt and undeterred by the fear of doing wrong; the best exemplar of that American statesmanship which accepted things as [Pg 113] they were and made the most of them. Facile, keen, effective, he had found life a series of opportunities easily embraced. Precocious in youth, marvelously active in manhood, he had learned without study, resolved without meditation, accomplished without toil. Whatever obstacles he had found in his path, he had either adroitly avoided them or boldly overleaped them, but never laboriously uprooted them. Whatever subject he had taken in hand, he had swiftly compassed it, but rarely probed to the heart of it. With books he dealt as he dealt with men, getting from them quickly what he liked or needed; he was as unlikely to pore over a volume, and dog-ear and annotate it, as he was with correspondence and slow talk and silences to draw out a friendship. Yet he was not cold or mean, but capable of hero-worship, following with ardor the careers of great conquerors like Cæsar and Napoleon, and capable, too, of loyalty to party and to men. He had great personal magnetism: young men, especially, he charmed and held as no other public man [Pg 114] could, now Clay was dead. His habits were convivial, and the vicious indulgence of his strong and masculine appetites, the only relaxation he craved in the intervals of his fierce activities, had caused him frequent illnesses; but he was still a young man, even by American standards, for the eminence he had attained. At the full of his extraordinary powers, battling for the high place he had and the higher he aspired to, there was nowhere to be seen his equal as a debater or a politician,—nowhere but in the ungainly figure, now once more erected into a posture of rivalry and defiance, of the man whom he had long ago outstripped and left behind him in the home of their common beginnings.

Slower of growth, and devoid altogether of many brilliant qualities which his rival possessed, Lincoln nevertheless outreached him by the measure of the two gifts the other lacked: the twin gifts of humor and of brooding melancholy. Bottomed by the one in homeliness, his character was by the other drawn upward to the height of human nobility and aspiration. His great capacity of pain, [Pg 115] which but for his buffoonery would no doubt have made him mad, was the source of his rarest excellencies. Familiar with squalor, and hospitable to vulgarity, his mind was yet tenanted by sorrow, a place of midnight wrestlings. In him, as never before in any other man, were high and low things mated, and awkwardness and ungainliness and uncouthness justified in their uses. At once coarser than his rival and infinitely more refined and gentle, he had mastered lessons which the other had never found the need of learning, or else had learned too readily and then dismissed. He had thoroughness for the other's competence; insight into human nature, and a vast sympathy, for the other's facile handling of men; a deep devotion to the right for the other's loyalty to party platforms. The very core of his nature was truth, and he himself is reported to have said of Douglas that he cared less for the truth, as the truth, than any other man he knew.

Hanging for some years upon the heels of his rival's rapid ascent, Lincoln had entered [Pg 116] the House as Douglas left it for the Senate, but at the end of the term he retired from politics baffled and discouraged. Tortured with the keen apprehension of a form and grace into which he could never mould his crudeness, tantalized with a sense that there must be a way for him to get a hold on his fellows and make a figure in the history of his times, he had watched the power of Douglas grow and the fame of Douglas spread until it seemed that Douglas's voice was always speaking and Douglas's hand was everywhere. Patiently working out the right and wrong of the fateful question Douglas dealt with so boldly, he came into the impregnable position of such as hated slavery and yet forbore to violate its sanctuary. Suddenly, with the repeal of the Missouri Compromise, Douglas himself had opened a path for him. He went back into politics, and took a leading part in the Anti-Nebraska movement. Whenever opportunity offered, he combated Douglas on the stump. The year Trumbull won the senatorship, Lincoln had first come within a few votes of it. Risen now to the [Pg 117] leadership of the Republicans in Illinois, he awaited Douglas at Chicago, listened to his opening speech, answered it the next evening, followed him into the centre of the State, and finally proposed a series of joint debates before the people. Douglas hesitated, but accepted, and named seven meeting-places: Ottawa and Freeport, in the northern stronghold of the Republicans; Galesburg, Quincy, and Charleston, in a region where both parties had a good following; and Jonesboro and Alton, which were in "Egypt." The first meeting was at Ottawa, in August; the last, at Alton, in the middle of October. Meanwhile, both spoke incessantly at other places, Douglas oftener than once a day. First the fame of Douglas, and then Lincoln's unexpected survival of the early meetings, drew the eyes of the whole country upon these two foremost Americans of their generation, face to face there on the Western prairie, fighting out the great question of the times.

Elevated side by side on wooden platforms in the open air, thrown into relief [Pg 118] against the low prairie sky line, the two figures take strong hold upon the imagination: the one lean, long-limbed, uncommonly tall; the other scarce five feet high, but compact, manful, instinct with energy, and topped with its massive head. In voice and gesture and manner, Douglas was incomparably the superior, as he was, too, in the ready command of a language never, indeed, ornate or imaginative, and sometimes of the quality of political commonplace, but always forcible and always intelligible to his audience. Lincoln had the sense of words, the imagination, the intensity of feeling, which go to the making of great literature; but for his masterpieces he always needed time. His voice was high and strained, his gestures ungraceful, his manner painful, save in the recital of those passages which he had carefully prepared or when he was freed of his self-consciousness by anger or enthusiasm. Neither of them, in any single speech, could be compared to

Webster in the other of the two most famous American debates, but the series was a remarkable exhibition of forensic [Pg 119] power. The interest grew as the struggle lengthened. People traveled great distances to hear them. At every meeting-place, a multitude of farmers and dwellers in country towns, with here and there a sprinkling of city-folk, crowded about the stand where "Old Abe" and the "Little Giant" turned and twisted and fenced for an opening, grappled and drew apart, clinched and strained and staggered,—but neither fell. The wonder grew that Lincoln stood up so well under the onslaughts of Douglas, at once skillful and reckless, held him off with so firm a hand, gripped him so shrewdly. Now, the wonder is that Douglas, wrestling with the man and the cause of a century, kept his feet and held his own.

He was fighting, too, with an enemy in the rear. When he turned to strike at the administration, Lincoln would call out: "Go it, husband! Go it, bear!" Apart from that diversion, however, the debate, long and involved as it was, followed but three general lines. The whole is resolvable [Pg 120] into three elements,—personalities, politics, and principles. There were the attacks which each made upon the other's record; the efforts which each made to weaken the other's position before the people; and the contrary views which were advanced.

Douglas began, indeed, with gracious compliments to his opponent, calling him "an amiable, kindly, and intelligent gentleman." Lincoln, unused to praise from such a source, protested he was like the Hoosier with the gingerbread: "He reckoned he liked it better than any other man, and got less of it." But in a moment Douglas was charging that Lincoln and Trumbull, Whig and Democrat, had made a coalition in 1854 to form the Black Republican party and get for themselves the two senatorships from Illinois, and that Trumbull had broken faith with Lincoln. Lincoln in turn made a charge that Douglas had conspired with Presidents Pierce and Buchanan and Chief Justice Taney to spread slavery and make it universal. The Kansas-Nebraska Act was their first step, the Dred Scott decision the [Pg 121] second; but one more step, and slavery could be fastened upon States as they had already fastened it upon Territories. Douglas protesting that to bring such a charge, incapable of proof or disproof, was indecent, Lincoln pointed out that Douglas had similarly charged the administration with conspiring to force a slave constitution upon Kansas; and afterwards took up a charge of Trumbull's that Douglas himself had at first conspired with Toombs and other senators to prevent any reference to the people of whatsoever constitution the Kansas convention might adopt. When they moved southward, Douglas charged Lincoln with inconsistency in that he changed his stand to suit the leanings of different communities. Of all these charges and counter-charges, however, none was absolutely proved, and no one now believes those which Douglas brought. But he made them serve, and Lincoln's, though he sustained them with far better evidence, and pressed them home with a wonderful clearness of reasoning, — once, he actually threw his argument [Pg 122] into a syllogism, — did no great harm to Douglas.

It was Douglas, too, who began the sparring for a political advantage. He knew that Lincoln's following was heterogeneous. "Their principles," he jeered, "in the north are jet black, in the centre they are in color a decent mulatto, and in lower Egypt they are almost white." His aim, therefore, was to fix upon Lincoln such extreme views as would alarm the more moderate of his followers, since the extremists must take him perforce, as a choice of two evils, even though he fell far short of their radical standard. To this end, Douglas produced certain resolutions which purported to have been adopted by an Anti-Nebraska convention at Springfield in 1854, and would have held Lincoln responsible for them. In a series of questions, he asked whether Lincoln were still opposed to a fugitive slave law, to the admission of any more slave States, and to acquiring any more territory unless the Wilmot Proviso were applied to it, and if he were still for prohibiting slavery outright in all [Pg 123] the Territories and in the District of Columbia, and for prohibiting the interstate slave trade. It soon transpired that Lincoln was not present at the Springfield convention, and that the resolutions were not adopted there, but somewhere else, and Douglas had to defend himself against a charge of misrepresentation. Nevertheless, when they met the second time, at Freeport, Lincoln answered the questions. He admitted the right of the South to a fugitive slave law. He would favor abolition in the District only if it were gradual, compensated, and accomplished with the consent of the inhabitants. He was not sure of the right of Congress to prohibit the interstate slave trade. He would oppose the annexation of fresh territory if there were reason to believe it would tend to aggravate the slavery controversy. He could see no way to deny the people of a Territory if slavery were prohibited among them during their territorial life and they nevertheless asked to come into the Union as a slave State. These cautious and hesitating answers displeased the stalwart [Pg 124] anti-slavery men. Lincoln would go their lengths in but one particular: he was for prohibiting slavery outright in all the Territories.

Then he brought forward some questions for Douglas to answer. Would Douglas vote to admit Kansas with less than 93,000 inhabitants if she presented a free state constitution? Would he vote to acquire fresh territory without regard to its effect on the slavery dispute? If the Supreme Court should decide against the right of a State to prohibit slavery, would he acquiesce? "Can the people of a United States Territory, in any lawful way, against the wish of any citizen of the United States, exclude slavery from its limits prior to the formation of a state constitution?"

Douglas had no great difficulty with the first three questions, and the fourth—the second, as Lincoln read them—he had in fact answered several times already, and in a way to please the Democrats of Illinois. But Lincoln, contrary to the advice of his friends, pressed it on him again with a view to the "all hail hereafter," for it was meant [Pg 125] to bring out the inconsistency of the principle of popular sovereignty with the Dred Scott decision, and the difference between the Northern and the Southern Democrats. Douglas answered it as he had before. The people of a Territory, through their legislature, could by unfriendly laws, or merely by denying legislative protection, make it impossible for a slave-owner to hold his slaves among them, no matter what rights he might have under the Constitution. Lincoln declared that the answer was historically false, for slaves had been held in Territories in spite of unfriendly legislation, and pointed out that if the Dred Scott decision was right the members of a territorial legislature, when they took an oath to support the Constitution, bound themselves to grant slavery protection. Later, in a fifth and last question, he asked whether, in case the slave-owners of a Territory demanded of Congress protection for their property, Douglas would vote to give it to them. But Douglas fell back upon his old position that Congress had no right to intervene. He would not break with his [Pg 126] supporters in Illinois, but by his "Freeport Doctrine" of unfriendly legislation he had broken forever with the men who were now in control of his party in the Southern States.

It was Lincoln who took the aggressive on principles. A famous paragraph of his speech before the convention which nominated him began with the words: "'A house divided against itself cannot stand.' I believe this government cannot endure permanently half slave and half free." That was a direct challenge to Douglas and his whole plan with slavery, and throughout the debate, at every meeting, the doctrine of the divided house was attacked and defended. Douglas declared that Lincoln was inciting half his countrymen to make war upon the other half; that he went for uniformity of domestic institutions everywhere, instead of letting different communities manage their domestic affairs as they chose. But no, Lincoln protested, he was merely for resisting the spread of slavery and putting it in such a state that the public mind would rest in the hope of its ultimate extinction. "But why," cried [Pg 127] Douglas, "cannot this government go on as the fathers left it, as it has gone on for more than a century?" Lincoln met him on that ground, and had the better of him in discussing what the fathers meant concerning slavery. They did not mean, he argued, to leave it alone to grow and spread, for they prohibited it in the Northwest Territory, they left the word "slave" out of the Constitution in the hope of a time when there should be no slaves under the flag. Over the true meaning of the Declaration of Independence, however, Douglas had a certain advantage, for Lincoln found the difficulty which candid minds still find in applying the principle of equality to races of unequal strength. Douglas plainly declared that ours is a white man's government. Lincoln admitted such an inferiority in negroes as would forever prevent the two races from living together on terms of perfect social and political equality, and if there must be inequality he was in favor of his own race having the superior place. He could only contend, therefore, for the negro's equality in those rights which are [Pg 128] set forth in the Declaration. Douglas made the most of this, and of Lincoln's failure, through a neglect to study the

economic character of slavery, to show clearly how the mere restriction of it would lead to its extinction.

But Douglas did not, and perhaps he could not, follow Lincoln
when he passed from the Declaration and the Constitution to the
"higher law," from the question of rights to the question of right and
wrong; for there Lincoln rose not merely above Douglas, but above
all that sort of politics which both he and Douglas came out of.
There, indeed, was the true difference between these men and their
causes. Douglas seems to shrink backward into the past, and Lincoln to come nearer and grow larger as he proclaims it: "That is the
real issue. That is the issue which will continue in this country when
these poor tongues of Judge Douglas and myself shall be silent. It is
the eternal struggle between these two principles—right and
wrong—throughout the world."

[Pg 129]

Nevertheless, Douglas won the senatorship and kept his hold on
the Northern Democrats. Immediately, he made a visit to the South.
He got a hearing there, and so made good his boast that he could
proclaim his principles anywhere in the Union; but when he returned to Washington he found that the party caucus, controlled by
Buchanan and the Southerners, had deposed him from the chair-
manship of the Committee on Territories, which he had held so
many years, and from this time he was constantly engaged with the
enemies he had made by his course on Lecompton and by his Freeport Doctrine. His Northern opponents were no longer in his way.
He had overmatched Sumner and Seward in the Senate, and beaten
the administration, and held his own with Lincoln, but the unbend-
ing and relentless Southerners he could neither beat nor placate. It
was men like Jefferson Davis in the Senate, and Yancey at Southern
barbecues and conventions, who stood now between him and his
ambition. That very slave power which he had served so well was
upreared to crush [Pg 130] him because he had come to the limit of
his subserviency. His plan of squatter sovereignty had not got the
Southerners Kansas, or any other slave State, to balance California
and Minnesota and Oregon. They demanded of Congress positive
protection for slavery in the Territories. The most significant debate
of the session was between Douglas on the one side and a group of

Southern senators, led by Jefferson Davis, on the other. He stood up against them manfully, and told them frankly that not a single Northern State would vote for any candidate on their platform, and they as flatly informed him that he could not carry a single Southern State on his.

He was too good a politician to yield, even if there had been no other reason to stand firm, but continued to defend the only doctrine on which there was the slightest chance of beating the Republicans in the approaching election. One method he took to defend it was novel, but he has had many imitators among public men of a later day. He wrote out his argument for "Harper's," the most [Pg 131] popular magazine of the day. The article is not nearly so good reading as his speeches, but it was widely read. Judge Jeremiah Black, the Attorney-General of Buchanan's cabinet, made a reply to it, and Douglas rejoined; but little of value was added to the discussions in Congress and on the stump. The Southerners, however, would not take warning. As they saw their long ascendency in the government coming to an end, their demands rose higher. Some of them actually began to agitate for a revival of the African slave trade; and this also Douglas had to oppose. His following in the Senate was now reduced to two or three, and one of these, Broderick, of California, a brave and steadfast man, was first defeated by the Southern interest, and then slain in a duel. John Brown's invasion of Virginia somewhat offset the aggressions of the South; but that, too, might have gone for a warning. The elections in the autumn of 1859 were enough to show that the North was no longer disposed to forbearance with slavery. Douglas went as far as any man [Pg 132] in reason could go in denouncing John Brown and those who were thought to have set him on; and he supported a new plan for getting Cuba. But Davis, on the very eve of the Democratic convention at Charleston, was pressing upon the Senate a series of resolutions setting forth the extreme demand of the South concerning the Territories. He was as bitter toward Douglas as he was toward the Republicans. At Charleston, Yancey took the same tone with the convention.

Practically the whole mass of the Northern Democrats were for Douglas now, and the mass of Southern Democrats were against him. The party was divided, as the whole country was, by a line that ran from East to West. Yet it was felt that nothing but the success of that party would avert the danger of disunion, and the best judges were of opinion that it could not succeed with any other candidate than Douglas or any other platform than popular sovereignty. His managers at Charleston offered the Cincinnati platform of 1856, with the addition [Pg 133] of a demand for Cuba and an indorsement of the Dred Scott decision and of any future decisions of the Supreme Court on slavery in the Territories. But the Southerners would not yield a hair's breadth. Yancey, their orator, upbraided Douglas and his followers with cowardice because they did not dare to tell the North that slavery was right. In that strange way the question of right and wrong was forced again upon the man who strove to ignore it. Senator Pugh, of Ohio, spokesman for Douglas, answered the fire-eaters. "Gentlemen of the South," he cried, "you mistake us! You mistake us! We will not do it." The Douglas platform was adopted, and the men of the cotton States withdrew. On ballot after ballot, a majority of those who remained, and a majority of the whole convention, stood firm for Douglas, but it was decided that two thirds of the whole convention was required to nominate. Men who had followed his fortunes until his ambition was become their hope in life, wearied out with the long deferment, broke down and wept. Finally, [Pg 134] it was voted to adjourn to Baltimore. In the interval, Davis and Douglas fell once more into their bitter controversy in the Senate.

At Baltimore, a new set of delegates from the cotton States appeared in place of the seceders, but they were no sooner admitted than another group withdrew, and even Cushing, the chairman, left his seat and followed them. Douglas telegraphed his friends to sacrifice him if it were necessary to save his platform, but the rump convention adopted the platform and nominated him. The two groups of seceders united on the Yancey platform and on Breckinridge, of Kentucky, for a candidate. A new party of sincere but unpractical Union-savers took the field with John Bell, an old Whig, for a candidate, and a platform of patriotic platitudes. The Republicans, guided in ways they themselves did not understand, had put aside Seward and taken Lincoln to be their leader.

The rivals were again confronted, but on cruelly unequal terms. From the first, it [Pg 135] was clear that nearly the whole North was going Republican, and that the cotton States were for Breckinridge or disunion. Whatever chance Douglas had in the border States and in the Democratic States of the North was destroyed by the new party. But he knew he was at the head of the true party of Jefferson, he felt that the old Union would not stand if he was beaten. He was the leader of a forlorn hope, but he led it superbly well. He undertook a canvass of the country the like of which no candidate had ever made before. At the very outset of it he was called upon to show his colors in the greater strife that was to follow. At Norfolk, in Virginia, it was demanded of him to say whether the election of a Black Republican President would justify the Southern States in seceding. He answered, no. Pennsylvania was again the pivotal State, and at an election in October the Republicans carried it over all their opponents combined. Douglas was in Iowa when he heard the news. He said calmly to his companions: "Lincoln is the next President. [Pg 136] I have no hope and no destiny before me but to do my best to save the Union from overthrow. Now let us turn our course to the South"—and he proceeded through the border States straight to the heart of the kingdom of slavery and cotton. The day before the election, he spoke at Montgomery, Yancey's home; that night, he slept at Mobile. If in 1858 he was like Napoleon the afternoon of Marengo, now he was like Napoleon struggling backward in the darkness toward the lost field of Waterloo. There was a true dignity and a true patriotism in his appeal to his maddened countrymen not to lift their hands against the Union their fathers made:—

"Woodman, spare that tree!
Touch not a single bough."

An old soldier of the Confederacy, scarred with the wounds he took at Bull Run, looking back over a wasted life to the youth he sacrificed in that ill-starred cause, remembers now as he remembers nothing else of the whole year of revolution the last plea of Douglas for the old party, the old Constitution, the old Union.

[Pg 137]

He carried but one State outright, and got but twelve votes in the electoral college. Lincoln swept the North, Breckinridge the South, and Bell the border States. Nevertheless, in the popular vote, hopeless candidate that he was, he stood next to Lincoln, and none of his competitors had a following so evenly distributed throughout the whole country.

When all was over, he could not rest, for he was still the first man in Congress, but hurried back to Washington and joined in the anxious conferences of such as were striving for a peaceable settlement. When South Carolina seceded, he announced plainly enough that he did not believe in the right of secession or consider that there was any grievance sufficient to justify the act. But he was for concessions if they would save the country from civil war. Crittenden, of Kentucky, coming forward after the manner of Clay with a series of amendments to the Constitution, and another Committee of Thirteen being named, Douglas was ready to play the same part he had played in 1850. [Pg 138] But the plan could not pass the Senate, and one after another the cotton States followed South Carolina. Then he labored with the men of the border States, and broke his last lance with Breckinridge, who, when he ceased to be Vice-President, came down for a little while upon the floor as a senator to defend the men whom he was about to join in arms against their country. Douglas engaged him with all the old fire and force, and worsted him in the debate.

His bearing toward Lincoln was generous and manly. When Lincoln, rising to pronounce his first inaugural address, looked awkwardly about him for a place to bestow his hat that he might adjust his glasses to read those noble paragraphs, Douglas came forward and took it from his hand. The graceful courtesy won him praise; and that was his attitude toward the new administration. The day Sumter was fired on, he went to the President to offer his help and counsel. There is reason to believe that during those fearful early days of power and trial Lincoln came into a better opinion of his rival.

[Pg 139]

The help of Douglas was of moment, for he had the right to speak for the Democrats of the North. On his way homeward, he was everywhere besought to speak. Once, he was aroused from sleep to address an Ohio regiment marching to the front, and his great voice rolled down upon them, aligned beneath him in the darkness, a word of loyalty and courage. At Chicago he spoke firmly and finally, for himself and for his party. While the hope of compromise lingered, he had gone to the extreme of magnanimity, but the time for conciliation was past. "There can be no neutrals in this war," he said: "only patriots and traitors." They were the best words he could have spoken. They were the last he ever spoke to his countrymen, for at once he was stricken down with a swift and mortal illness and hurried to his end. A little while before the end, his wife bent over him for a message to his sons. He roused himself, and said: "Tell them to obey the laws and support the Constitution of the United States." He died on June 11, 1861, in the forty-ninth year of his age.

[Pg 140]

It was a hard time to die. War was at hand, and his strong nature stirred at the call. Plunged in his youth into affairs, and wonted all his life to action, he had played a man's part in great events, and greater were impending. He had taken many blows of men and circumstance, and stormy times might bring redress. He was a leader, and for want of him a great party must go leaderless and stumbling to a long series of defeats. He was a true American, and his country was in danger. He was ambitious, and his career was not rightly finished. He was the second man in the Republic, and he might yet be the first.

But first he never could have been while Lincoln lived, nor ever could have got a hold like Lincoln's on his kind. His place is secure among the venturesome, strong, self-reliant men who in various ages and countries have for a time hastened, or stayed, or diverted from its natural channel the great stream of affairs. The sin of his ambition is forgiven him for the good end he made. But for all his splendid energy and his [Pg 141] brilliant parts, for all the charm of his bold assault on fortune and his dauntless bearing in adversity, we cannot turn from him to his rival but with changed and softened eyes. For Lincoln, indeed, is one of the few men eminent in politics whom we admit into the hidden places of our thought; and there, released from that coarse clay which prisoned him, we companion him forever with the gentle and heroic of older lands. Douglas abides without.

The Riverside Press
Electrotyped and printed by H.O. Houghton & Co.
Cambridge, Mass., U.S.A.